Masterpieces of
URDU RUBAIYAT

This book contains English translations of 269 *rubaies*, chosen from the works of 25 famous poets, chronologically arranged. It covers a wide spectrum of Urdu poetry, from Mir and Sauda in the 18th century to Josh and Firaq in the 20th century. The criterion for selection is the intrinsic quality of a quatrain, determined by the universality of its theme, the depth of poetic perception, and the dexterity of expression. The book presents a rich and varied poetic fare. Those interested in philosophical or mystical thought will enjoy reading the *rubaies* of Dard, Anees, Dabir, or Amjad; those looking for the poetry of love and romance should read the quatrains of Momin, Firaq and Josh; while those fond of social satire and moral instruction may turn to Akbar, Hali, and Mehroom.

While translating the *rubaies* the author has taken care to preserve the sense and spirit, as also the rhyming pattern of the original. The language used in translation is lucid, poetical, and appropriately expressive. Each *rubai* is first presented in Urdu calligraphics; this is followed, on the opposite page, by its English translation, which, in turn, is succeeded by the Romanized version of the Urdu text. The introductory essay on Urdu *Rubai*, discussing the origin, development, and potentialities of this form, is an added attraction of the book.

K.C. Kanda has been, till recently, a senior lecturer in English at Bhagat Singh College, University of Delhi. He holds M.A.degrees in English from the Universities of Panjab and Nottingham (U.K.), a Ph.D in English and a first class Master's degree in Urdu from the University of Delhi. While English poetry has been his speciality professionally, Urdu poetry has been his love since his school days. He has made a deep study of Urdu poets, both ancient and modern, and is fully conversant with the subtleties of poetic art and thought.

Dr. Kanda has published a critical study of Tennyson's poetry entitled The Two Worlds of Tennyson, *and an* Anthology of English Poems. *He is the author of the bestseller*, Masterpieces of Urdu Ghazal: From 17th to 20th Century (Sterling publication). *He has also published articles on the poetry of Ghalib, Tennyson, and W.S.Blunt.*

Excerpts from the reviews

Masterpieces of Urdu Ghazal

"It is a miracle that despite the strait-jacket in which it was enclothed, the ghazal not only survived but flourished through the centuries.... I recommend this anthology to lovers of Urdu poetry."

—*Khushwant Singh, Sunday*

"All in all, it is a book for the shelves of both who know and love Urdu and would like to be conversant with its best form of poetry."

—*The Pioneer*

"Mr. Kanda in his well-researched volume has painstakingly brought out the best of Urdu Ghazal, and this concise volume could well be considered a boon for research scholars in Urdu poetry."

—*The Hindu*

Urdu Ghazals: An Anthology

"Mr. K.C. Kanda has painstakingly included in the Anthology an excellent selection of Urdu ghazals, not only in Urdu (Persian) script, the English translation of a high quality, but, more importantly, the transcription in Roman as well. The volume would rank high among other works of a similar nature."

—*The Hindu*

Masterpieces of Urdu Rubaiyat

This book contains English translations of 269 rubaies, chosen from the works of 25 famous poets, chronologically arranged. It covers a wide spectrum of Urdu poetry, from Mir and Sauda in the 18th century to Josh and Firaq in the 20th century.

—*Globe*

Masterpieces of Urdu Nazm

This book is intended to introduce the reader to the best specimens of the Urdu *nazm*, as distinguished from the *ghazal*. It contains English translations of 42 *nazms*, chosen from the works of 19 famous poets, such as Mir Taqi Mir, Nazir Akbarabadi, Shauq Lucknavi, Iqbal, Josh, Hafeez, Akhtar Sheerani, Majaaz, Faiz, and Sahir. The poets are presented in chronological order, and each is introduced with an authentic portrait, and a brief biographical-cum-critical note. The "Introduction" attempts in lucid prose a definition of the *nazm*, and describes its characteristic features as an art form.

Published by
Sterling Publishers Private Limited

Masterpieces of
URDU RUBAIYAT

K.C. KANDA

A Sterling Paperback

STERLING PAPERBACKS
An imprint of
Sterling Publishers (P) Ltd.
A-59 Okhla Industrial Area, Phase-II,
New Delhi-110020.
Tel: 6313023, 6320118, 6916165, 6916209
Fax: 91-11-6331241   E-mail: ghai@nde.vsnl.net.in
www.sterlingpublishers.com

Masterpieces of Urdu Rubaiyat
© 1995, K.C. Kanda
ISBN 81 207 1827 5
Reprint 1996, 2001

All rights are reserved. No part of this publication may be reproduced, stored in a retrieval system or transmitted, in any form or by any means, mechanical, photocopying, recording or otherwise, without prior written permission of the original publisher.

Published by Sterling Publishers Pvt. Ltd., New Delhi-110 020.
Printed at Ram Printograph (India), Delhi-110051.
Cover design by Biplab

To My Wife
SNEH

تو ہاتھ کو جب ہاتھ میں لے لیتی ہے
دکھ درد زمانے کے مٹا دیتی ہے
سنسار کے اس تپتے ہوئے ویرانے میں
سکھ شانت کی گویا تو ہری کھیتی ہے

When, my Love, you hold my hand,
Hordes of sorrows you disband;
In this world's burning wild,
Green, oasis-like, you stand.

Tu haath ko jab haath mein le leti hai,
Dukh dard zamaane ke mita deti hai;
Sansaar ke is tapte hue veeraane mein,
Sukh shaant ki goya tu hari kheti hai.

Firaq

PREFACE

This book is a sequel to my earlier work, *Masterpieces of Urdu Ghazal*, published in 1990. The *rubai*, as most of us know, is a frequent companion to the *ghazal*, often used by poets and singers, at public symposia, as a prelude to their longer compositions. This poetic form is ideally suited to serve the twin purposes of delight and instruction. Because of its brevity, pointedness, and musicality, it makes an instant appeal to the reader's mind and sinks deep into his memory. Urdu poetry contains a rich stock of *rubaies*, remarkable for the beauty and variety of their theme and style, deserving, as such, to be treasured and translated into a language which enjoys a much wider currency than Urdu. I have put together in the following pages 272 *rubaies* carefully selected from the works of 25 famous poets, covering a vast spectrum of Urdu poetry, from Mir and Sauda in the 18th century to Josh and Firaq in the 20th. The poets who have specialised in this *genre*, such as Anees, Dabir, Amjad, Josh and Firaq, are, appropriately, given a greater representation than their less distinguished compeers. In the case of such master-poets as Mir, Ghalib or Faiz, who are not exclusively the poets of this form, I have included, along with their *rubaiyat*, some of their *qitaat*, for a *qita*, though technically different from the *rubai*, vies with it in its total poetic effect. As the book is meant to cater to readers of all tastes, I have seen to it that the *rubaies* presented here possess a universality of appeal, by virtue of their content and style. Many of these, I am sure, are already familiar to the lovers of Urdu poetry.

While translating these quatrains I have taken care to preserve the sense and spirit of the original, though it may involve an occasional departure from the literal accuracy of the text. I have also adhered to the rhyming pattern of the *rubai*, but where a suitable rhyming word eluded my grasp, I haven't hesitated to use assonance in place of rhyme. The language used for translation is, on the whole, lucid, rhythmical and adequately expressive, not only of the meaning, but also, as far as possible, of the melody of the original.

Paradoxical as it may seem, while there has been a perceptible increase in the popularity of Urdu poetry, be it the *ghazal*, or the *rubai*, there is a palpable decline in the number of those who can read and understand Urdu in the Persian script. For the benefit of those who would like to have a feel of the Urdu language without being conversant with the script, I have provided Romanized versions of the Urdu text. Each *rubai* is first given in the Urdu script. This is followed, on the opposite page, by its English translation, which, in turn, is succeeded by the Romanised version, in italics. I have also added an introductory essay which discusses the origin, development and potentialities of this form, and examines, with suitable illustrations, the salient characteristics of its renowned practitioners.

I am again grateful to Dr. J.S. Neki, who, as in the case of the *Masterpieces of Urdu Ghazal*, perused these pages with a loving care and made many useful suggestions. Dr. Neki is a rare combination of a poet and a scientist; he is a psychiatrist not only of the mind, but also of the heart and soul. Reading and revising these quatrains in his company has been a source of rare delight. I am beholden to Professor Gopi Chand Narang whose advice and encouragement have gone a long way in the successful completion of this work. His sound and scholarly judgement helped me in choosing the poets, and his personal library provided me with the necessary background information, used in the Introduction. Thanks are also due to Mr. Daleep Badal, a talented Urdu poet, who patiently read through these quatrains and suggested several improvements. For my source of original material, I have drawn mainly on the Delhi University Library (North Campus). I am lucky to include among my friends three officers of the library—Mr. M.L. Saini, Mr. N.A. Abbasi, and Mr. R.C. Chhiber—who are keenly interested in English and Urdu literature. I am extremely grateful to them for their willing counsel and cooperation. Further, I am grateful to Mr. Ali Siddiqui, Founder and Organizing Secretary of Aalami Urdu Conference, for allowing me to reproduce some of the pictures of the Urdu poets contained in the art gallery of "Urdu Morcha." I must also express my sense of affectionate appreciation to my son, Dr. Arun Kanda, who, as before, carefully scanned the manuscript and corrected many typographical errors. Last, though by no means least, I am thankful to Mr. S.K. Ghai of *Sterling Publishers* who readily agreed to publish this book.

K.C.K.

CONTENTS

	Preface	vii
1.	INTRODUCTION: FORM AND FEATURES OF URDU RUBAI	1
2.	MIRZA MOHAMMED RAFI SAUDA (1713-1781)	25
3.	KHWAJA MIR DARD (1720-1784)	31
4.	MIR TAQI MIR (1722-1808)	37
5.	QALANDAR BAKHSH JURRAT (1748-1809)	51
6.	BAHADUR SHAH ZAFAR (1775-1869)	53
7.	SHEIKH MOHAMMED IBRAHIM ZAUQ (1789-1854)	57
8.	MIRZA ASADULLAH KHAN GHALIB (1797-1869)	63
9.	MOMIN KHAN MOMIN (1800-1852)	67
10.	MIRZA SALAMAT ALI DABIR (1803-1875)	75
11.	MIR BABAR ALI ANEES (1804-1874)	85
12.	ABDUL ALEEM AASI GHAZIPURI (1834-1917)	93
13.	KHWAJA ALTAF HUSSAIN HALI (1837-1914)	97
14.	AKBAR HUSSAIN KHAN AKBAR ALLAHABADI (1846-1921)	107
15.	SAYED ALI MOHAMMED SHAD AZIMABADI (1846-1927)	113

16.	SURAJ NARAIN MEHAR (1859-1931)	121
17.	SAYED AHMED HUSSAIN AMJAD HYDERABADI (1878-1961)	123
18.	SHAUKAT ALI KHAN FANI BADAYUNI (1879-1941)	133
19.	YAAS YAGANA CHANGEZI (1884-1956)	139
20.	LABHU RAM JOSH MALSIANI (1884-1976)	143
21.	TILOK CHAND MEHROOM (1887-1965)	147
22.	JAGAT MOHAN LAL RAWAN (1889-1934)	153
23.	RAGHUPATI SAHAI FIRAQ GORAKHPURI (1896-1982)	161
24.	SHABBIR HASAN KHAN JOSH MALIHABADI (1898-1982)	173
25.	FAIZ AHMED FAIZ (1911-1984)	195
26.	NARESH KUMAR SHAD (1927-1969)	205

INTRODUCTION
Form and Features of Urdu *Rubai*

The *rubai* is a fascinating poetic form, compact in size, yet sufficiently capacious to give a telling aesthetic expression to the poet's insights and experiences. Though not as popular nor as widely practised as the *ghazal*, the *rubai* is a frequent companion to the *ghazal*, often used by poets and singers as a prelude to their longer compositions for setting the tone and whetting the appetite of their audience. That the form has a strong appeal for the lovers of poetry was proved, long ago, by Edward Fitzgerald (1809-83), whose translation of *The Rubaiyat of Omar Khayyam,* published in 1859, had won uncommon acclaim from its Victorian readers. Fitzgerald's version was instrumental in introducing the English-knowing readers to the form and flavour of the *rubai*, ensuring, in the process, its recognition as an important literary form.

The word *rubai*, like *ghazal*, is an Arabic word, derived from "rubaa", or "arbaa" meaning "four". In poetic parlance, the *rubai* is an independent quatrain, a four-lined stanza rhyming aaba. Each line of the quatrain conforms to a specific poetic measure called *hazaj*, consisting of four metrical units, represented in prosodic terms by the Persian notation: mufailun, mufailun, mufailun, mufailun; or by one of its twenty-four variants. The famous Arabic exclamation, "Lahaul willa qwatta ill billa," represents, in a practical form, one of the accepted metres of the *rubai*, and is sometimes used as a ready-reckoner, a rough metrical yardstick, by students of prosody. Recognising the difficulty of transferring the complicated metre of the original into English, Fitzgerald is content to substitute for the Persian metre the five-foot iambic quatrain as exemplifed below:

Ah Love! could thou and I with Fate conspire
To grasp this sorry scheme of Things entire,
Would not we shatter it to bits—and then
Re-mould it nearer to the Heart's desire!

Fitzgerald is, however, careful to preserve the rhyming pattern of the original, attempting thereby to recapture some of the Oriental melody. The four-lined stanza, rhyming aaba, is a novelty in English verse. English poets have frequently used the iambic quatrain, sometimes of the enclosed type, as in Tennyson's *In Memoriam*, and sometimes with alternating rhyming pattern, as in Gray's "An Elegy Written in a Country Churchyard", but we rarely come across an iambic quatrain with the rhyme scheme of the *rubai*. The main strength of this quatrain resides in its last line, which, repeating the rhyme of the first two lines, clinches the issue with a final, finishing stroke. The first two lines introduce the topic and kindle the reader's curiosity about the main drive of the poet. The third line, moving with a relatively easy pace, sharpens the edge of the reader's curiosity and increases his suspense, so that the reader, like a swimmer about to make his plunge, awaits, with baited breath, the outcome of his poetic encounter— the outcome which is emphatically conveyed in the quintessential fourth line. An Urdu poet, Hamid Hussain Qadiri has underscored the importance of the last line of the *rubai* with the aid of a sacred allusion. While paying a tribute to the unmatched glory of the Prophet, he has also placed the *rubai's* concluding line on the highest pedestal:

دنیا میں رسول اور بھی لاکھ سہی
زیبا ہے مگر حضور کو تاج سہی
ہے خاتمۂ حسن عناصر اں پسر
ہیں مصرعۂ آخر اس رباعی کے وہی

With prophets unnumbered let the world abound,
Your Grace alone deserves to be regally crowned;
You represent the ultimate in the elements'
  beauteous blend,
You are the *rubai's* last line, complete in sense and
  sound.

And Firaq Gorakhpuri, a twentieth century master of the Urdu *rubai* has described, in his own sensuous way, the interlinked sweetness of the four lines:

پہلے مصرعے میں حسن کا خطۂ جبیں
اور دوسرے میں لٹوں کی تنزئیں
چوتھا ہو نکلتا ہُوا یوں تیسرے سے
جیسے بھیگی مسیں ہوں ابرو سے حسیں

The first line should reflect the beauty's perfect brow,
The second portray the sable locks aglow,
The fourth from the third should thus seem to flow,
As the greening upper lip from the arched eyebrow.

Apart from suggesting Firaq's characteristic fondness for lingering luxuriously on the sensuous charms of beauty, the foregoing quatrain brings out the importance of thematic unity and continuity in a *rubai*, which aspect distinguishes it from the *ghazal*, where the different couplets are often independent of each other in regard to their thought-content.

Another poetic form in Urdu called *qita* is a near approximation to the *rubai*. It generally (though not always) consists of four lines, and obeys the law of thematic unity and consistency, containing the complete expression of a single idea or emotion. But it is not governed by the metrical restrictions of the *rubai*, nor does it follow the *rubai's* rhyme scheme. We may have a *qita* with all the four lines rhyming together, or one in which only the second and fourth line rhyme. Yet in its total poetic effect, the *qita* is not different from the *rubai*, so much so that the common reader who is indifferent to the technicalities of the poetic form finds the two kinds indistinguishable. It is interesting to remember that Harivansh Rai Bachchan's Hindi composition, "Madhushala" (1935) which generally passes as a sequence of *rubaiyat* in the manner of Khayyam, is, in fact, a collection of *qitas*, generally rhyming a b a b. In view of the proximity of the two forms, I have taken the liberty, in the following pages, to include a sprinkling of *qitas* in the midst of *rubaies*, taking care that the *qitas* so chosen are intrinsically and poetically satisfying.

The *rubai* has some broad resemblance to the English sonnet, which, though, three and a half times longer than the *rubai*, embodies the expression of a single idea, emotion, or situation, introduced, generally in the octave, and concluded, often with a touch of surprise, in the sestet, or in the concluding couplet of a Shakespearean sonnet. The last line of the *rubai* recalls at times the last line of a Miltonic sonnet, or the concluding couplet of a Shakespearean sonnet. The discipline of metre, rhyme and length, essential for the *rubai*, is also obligatory for the sonnet, though the two forms of the sonnet, Italian and Shakespearean, observe different rhyming patterns. Also, quite a few *rubaies* in Urdu begin, like some sonnets of Shakespeare, Milton, or Keats, with the adverb "when", and conclude with the answering "then", more often implied than stated. But we cannot press the comparison too far. The *rubai* has a much narrower canvas than the sonnet. The poet of the *rubai* has to present in just four lines what a sonneteer can debate and discuss in fourteen lines. Consequently, he has to do with symbol and suggestion what a sonneteer does with descriptive or narrative detail. For example, when

Shakespeare is to pay a tribute to the remarkable powers of love and friendship in his sonnet, "When to the Sessions of Sweet Silent Thought", he piles sorrow upon sorrow in the first three quatrains, and then suddenly reverses the effect, and routs the forces of darkness with the overwhelming light and warmth of love, condensed in the concluding couplet:

> But when the while I think on thee, dear friend,
> All losses are restored and sorrows end.

As against this, when Firaq Gorakhpuri treats the same theme in the mould of the *rubai*, he dispenses with descriptive detail, and exploits instead the resources of appropriately expressive imagery:

تو ہاتھ کو جب ہاتھ میں لے لیتی ہے
دکھ درد زمانے کے مٹا دیتی ہے
سنسار کے تپتے ہوئے ویرانے میں
سکھ شانت کی گویا تو ہری کھیتی ہے

> When, my Love, you hold my hand,
> Hordes of sorrows you disband,
> In this world's burning wild,
> Green, oasis-like you stand.

The Hindi verse form called "chaupai", could be called a near parallel to the *rubai*. The "chaupai", as the name suggests, is a poetical unit of four lines, but it is not always a self-sufficient unit like the *rubai*, and is often used, as in Tulsi Das's *Ramayana*, as a medium of long narrative poem, which is not the case with the *rubai*. Moreover, the rhyme scheme of the "chaupai" is different from that of the *rubai*, for it generally contains two couplets with two different rhyme schemes. It would seem that apart from the similarity of nomenclature and the number of lines, the two forms, *rubai* and *chaupai*, are essentially different.

The brevity of space, combined with the restraints of metre and rhyme, makes the task of the writer of the *rubai* comparatively difficult, so much so that even master poets like Ghalib and Zauq, it is pointed out by a literary critic,* have at times faltered in the handling of this form. And yet, the brevity, pointedness and musicality of the *rubai* are among its chief attractions.

There is an interesting Persian legend relating to the origin of the *rubai*. One day, a small boy, the son of Amir Saffaar of Ghazni (died 265 Hijri), was playing walnuts with his friends. He was aiming to put the walnuts into a hole in the ground. Seven of his walnuts rolled down into the hole, but the last one trailed leisurely behind. After a while the last walnut too moved reluctantly onwards and tumbled into the hole. The boy felt excited and exclaimed: "Ghaltaan, ghaltaan, hami rud ta lab-e-goo" (Halting, faltering, all have stumbled into the hole). This remark was overheard by Rodki, the famous Persian poet, who, finding the line perfectly poetical, and in metrical conformity with the popular four-unit measure called "Hazaj" added three more lines to it in the same metre, and turned it into the first Persian *rubai*.

According to another version, it was not Rodki, but two Arab poets, Abudalf, and Zeenat-ul-Kaab, who, impressed by the boy's spontaneous utterance, supplied the three additional lines, and produced the first *rubai*. Firman Fatehpuri, the author of *Urdu Rubai*,** questions the authenticity of the above legend. If Rodki, he argues, is to be linked with the popular legend, he should have lived in the time of Amir Yaqub Saffaar, which is historically incorrect. Saffaar died in 265 Hijri, while Rodki died 6 decades later in 329 Hijri (A.D. 910). Thus Rodki could not have been commissioned by the Amir to examine the line of his son, and produce three more lines in the same metre. Firman Fatehpuri also rejects the claim of the aforesaid Arab poets on the

---
* Firman Fatehpuri, *Urdu Rubai*, Modern Publishers, Karachi, 1962, pp. 64, 65.
** ibid., p. 45.

ground that the *rubai* is a Persian rather than an Arabic verse form. Rodki, the Persian poet, was no doubt fully competent to experiment with the new verse forms, but the scholars have not been able to trace any *rubai* which could be authentically linked with his name. In the face of these uncertainties, it is safer to assume that the *rubai* was not invented by a particular poet, but evolved out of the earlier Persian poetic forms of "do-beiti" (the term literally means a stanza of two couplets or four lines), or "tarana". The "tarana", so called presumably because of its singing quality, is a self-sufficient quatrain like the *rubai*, but it is not bound by the metrical restrictions or the rhyme scheme of the *rubai*. Generally, in a "tarana" all the four lines rhyme together. According to Dr. Sir Mohd Iqbal "do-beiti", or "tarana", became a *rubai* when the third line dispensed with the rhyme.* However we do come across *rubaies* with all the four lines rhyming together. Such *rubaies* are technically called "Khassi", as against the "Ghair-Khassi" *rubaies*, of the accepted rhyming order. When each line of the *rubai* is extended by adding to it a short sentence on the same rhyme, we get a new brand of *rubai* called, "mastzaad".**

Though the *rubai* took its birth in the 10th century Iran, in the time of Rodki, it attained popularity and perfection in the 11th century, when three famous poets, Abu Sayed Abu-ul-Khair, Omar Khayyam, and Sarmad contributed to the enrichment of this form. While Abu-ul-Khair dealt predominantly with mystical and moral themes, Omar Khayyam and Sarmad expanded the scope of this form by expressing in their *rubaies* philosophic, romantic and bacchanalian themes. With the advent of the Muslims in the 13th century, the *rubai*, along with the other poetic "kinds", such as "qasida", "ghazal",

---

*   See *Nectar of Grace—Omar Khayyam's Life and Works*, Swami Govinda Tirath, Kitabistan, Allahabad, 1941, p. cxxxiv.
** See Mir Taqi Mir's last *rubai* in this collection.

"masnavi", or "marsia", was transplanted from Iran to India. But it did not immediately excite the imagination of the Urdu poets who were, generally, engaged in practising the other poetic forms like "masnavi", "qasida", or "ghazal". The complete works of Mohd. Quli Qutab Shah (973-1020 Hijri), which contain about 50,000 couplets, also include, in addition to other genres, 41 *rubaies*, none of which can, however, be called particularly distinguished. We may read the following *rubai* as a specimen, where Qutab Shah is thinking of the uniqueness of the Creator:

تجھ حسن سے تازہ ہے سدا حسن و جمال
تجھ یاد کی مستی اے عشق کوں حال
تو ایک ہے تجھ سا نہیں دوجا کوئی،
کیوں پاوے جگت صفحے میں کوئی تیری مثال

All beauty on this earth derives its freshness from Thy grace,
Thy intoxicating thought causes love's ecstatic state;
Unique you are in the world, without a match or peer,
How can we find anywhere Thy mate or duplicate?

The other important poets of the Deccan School, Mulha Wajhi, Wali, and Siraj also tried their hand at the *rubai*, though the form was never their forte.

As we approach the poets of the Delhi School, we can see a definite development of the *rubai* in the skilled hands of men like Mir Dard (1720-1784), Mir Taqi Mir (1722-1808), and Mirza Sauda (1713-1781). Out of these Dard is ranked higher than Mir and Sauda in the field of the *rubai*, though as a writer of the *ghazal* he does not measure up to them. As in his *ghazals* so in his *rubaies*, Dard is primarily concerned with mystic and moral themes, but his true greatness lies in his ability to transmute mystical thought into poetry, and to present transcendental love through the idiom of earthly love.

This makes him enjoyable both in the religious and secular circles. In the following *rubai* Dard is reflecting upon the predicament of man who is caught between the conflicting claims of sense and spirit, hell and heaven:

پیدا کرے ہر چند تقدّس بندہ
مشکل ہے کہ حرص سے ہو دل برکندہ
جنت میں بھی اکل و شرب سے نہیں ہے نجات
دوزخ کا بہشت میں بھی ہوگا دھندا

Let a man try his best to cleanse and purify,
Never can he purge his heart of the lusts of life;
No escape from sensuous feast even in Paradise,
Even the holy heaven, paths of hell provides.

Mir Taqi Mir imparts to his *rubaies* the same pathos and compassion which is the hallmark of his *ghazals*. His *rubaies* and *qitas* are also notable for the beauty of their style, for their conversational flow, naturalness of diction, and a haunting sweetness. Here is a specimen of his characteristic mood and manner:

لوگ بہت پوچھا کرتے ہیں کیا کہئے میاں کیا ہے عشق
کچھ کہتے ہیں سر التفی، کچھ کہتے ہیں، خدا ہے عشق
الفت سے پرہیز کیا کر، کلفت اس میں نہایت ہے
یعنی درد و رنج و تعب ہے آفتِ جاں ہے، بلا ہے عشق

Often do the people ask, what is love? who can explain?
For some it's the fount divine, by some it's God proclaimed;
You should beware of love, it causes endless pain,
Sorrow, suffering, terror, torture—love is known by many a name.

Sauda's *rubaies* are cunningly wrought. Though he treats the stock themes of the transience of life, importance of love, or the compulsions of man, he presents his themes with the aid of ingenious similes and learned diction, so as to make them typically distinctive:

بوؤں میں تخمِ گل کو جہاں واں زقوم ہو
پالوں جو عندلیب قفس میں تو بوم ہو
اپنے چمن کو فائدہ کیا تجھ سے اے صبا
یہ جا ہے کہ یاں دمِ عیسیٰ سموم ہو

If I sow the seeds of flowers, nettle only grow,
A nightingale by me encaged becomes an owl, I trow;
What good to my garden can you cause, O breeze?
Scorching like the simoom here, the breath of Christ doth blow.

Among the next triumvirate of poets—Ghalib (1797-1869), Zauq (1789-1854), and Momin (1801-1852)—who reigned the Delhi school of poetry in the last phase of the Moghul Empire, and lent to their age an imperishable glory by their poetic exertions, Momin alone expended time and talent on the cultivation of the *rubai*. His complete works contain about 150 *rubaies* covering a vast range of subjects including love and romance, philosophy, morality, religion, or social satire. However, it is as a poet of love, love real and earthy, that Momin is most effective. He had a rich personal experience of romantic love, which lies skilfully distilled in his *rubaies*. In the following example Momin is pondering over the eternal dilemma of desire and discipline:

یہ حکمِ خدا کا کہ قطرے کا نہ پیوں
اور مرضیِ جاناں کہ پیمانہ پیوں
تو بھی ہے عزیز، خاطرِ ساقی بھی
حیراں ہوں کہ پھر بادہ پیوں یا نہ پیوں

God forbids me to drink even a little drop,
Saqi wants I should drain away the draught,
I respect my Saqi, I revere my God,
To drink or not to drink, how should I resolve?

Ghalib paid but scant attention to this form, and among the few *rubaies* found in his Dewan, none is really distinguished. Zauq's performance in this domain is better than that of Ghalib. Zauq's output is not impressive quantitatively; he wrote no more than 16 or 17 *rubaies* but some of his *rubaies* are still remembered for the universality of their thought, for their speech-like rhythms, and for the aptness of word and phrase. However, it may be added as a footnote that it was not because of a deficient poetic capability that Ghalib didn't excel in this field. One can surmise that his more serious preoccupation with the *ghazal* left him little time or inclination to nurture the less important form of the *rubai*. The following quatrain of Ghalib contains sufficient evidence of his artistic and imaginative ability:

گھر ہمارا جو نہ روتے تو بھی ویران ہوتا
بحر گر بحر نہ ہوتا تو بیاباں ہوتا
تنگی دل کا گلہ کیسا یہ وہ کافر دل ہے
کہ گر تنگ نہ ہوتا تو پریشاں ہوتا

My home would have been wrecked, even if I hadn't wept,
Had the sea been not the sea, desert would have therein crept;
Rue not its narrowness; this infidel heart
Had it not been narrow, would have been perplexed.

In the above quatrain the poet is making the proverbial two voyages—the voyage within, into the realm of the human heart, and the voyage without, to the world of earth and ocean. The second line of the quatrain, "Had the sea been not the sea, desert would have therein crept," shows Ghalib's awareness of the facts of geology and evolutionary thought which were agitating the minds of poets and thinkers in the contemporary West. One is reminded of Tennyson's famous quatrain in *In Memoriam*, where he is brooding over the phenomenon of change constantly operative in the physical world:

> There rolls the deep where grew the tree,
> O Earth, what changes hast thou seen,
> There where the long street roars, has been
> The stillness of the central sea.
>
> (I.M., CXXII)

A reference to the ceaseless process of change is also contained in one of the *rubaies* of Bahadur Shah Zafar, the poet-emperor, contemporaneous with Ghalib:

کتنے ہی بن کے شہر کے اور گاؤں کے نشاں
یوں مٹ گئے زمیں پہ کہ یوں پاؤں کے نشاں
گر نخلِ خشک کوئی کہیں رہ گیا طُفَ
پائے نہ اس کے پاؤں تلے چھاؤں کے نشاں

Many a mark of town and village, many a mark of waste,
Have faded like footprints from the earth's face,
If at all a withered trunk somewhere you espy,
In vain you'll look beneath, for a trace of shade.

The foregoing *rubaies* of Ghalib and Zafar also indicate that the thematic scope of the *rubai* has by now been considerably improved, for in addition to the favourite themes of love, mysticism and morality, the rubai has also drawn in its ambit some of the prevalent scientific thinking of the day—though by its very nature and size, it can provide only a hint, and not a detailed discussion of these ideas.

While the famous 19th century poets of the Delhi

School—with the exception of Momin—made no serious attempt to cultivate the *rubai*, the Lucknow school of poetry produced two important poets, Anees (1804-1874) and Dabir (1803-1875), both contemporaries of Ghalib, who, aside from specialising as writers of "marsias" (elegies), made a remarkable contribution to the development of this form. Anees wrote nearly 550 *rubaies*, while Dabir has about 200 *rubaies* to his credit. The *rubaies* of both these poets, separated from their complete works, have since been published in the book form, and have been critically evaluated. Because of their deeply religious commitment, their *rubaies* possess a seriousness of purpose with a commensurate sobriety of style. They have also introduced into their *rubaies* some of the sacred events and allusions of the battle of Karbala, highlighting, in the process, the virtues of valour, loyalty, self-sacrifice, truthfulness and the like. But while this emphasis on the serious and sacred aspects of life invests their compositions with a strong moral fibre, it deprives them of colour and liveliness which account for the continued popularity of romantic and bacchanalian verse. Consequently, only those *rubaies* of Anees and Dabir are read and remembered by the average reader which deal with universal themes and are unencumbered with esoteric thought and references. The chief merits of their best *rubaies* lie in their thoughtful and thought-provoking content, in their unaffected diction, in their natural rhythmic flow, and in the solemnity of their tone. The following quotations will illustrate their characteristic tone and temper:

سینے میں یہ دم شمع سحر گاہی ہے
جو ہے اس کارواں میں وہ راہی ہے
پیچھے کبھی قافلہ سے رہتا نہ انیسؔ
اے عمرِ دراز تیری کوتاہی ہے

The breath within the breast is the flickering lamp of dawn,
Travellers are we all who form this caravan,
Anees would never have lagged behind his mates,
Because of you, O long life, he trails the marathon.

Anees

پہونچا جو کمال کو وطن سے نکلا
قطرہ جو گوہر بنا عدن سے نکلا
تکمیل کمال کی غریبی ہے دلیل
پختہ جو ثمر ہوا چمن سے نکلا

You are externed from home when excellence you hit,
The drop turned a pearl its Aden has to quit,
Perfect talent necessitates exile from home,
When the fruit is ripe, it's poised for exit.

Dabir

To these two poets also goes the credit of popularising the *rubai* in social and literary circles. Anees, in particular, started the practice of introducing his longer poems, his 'masnavies' and 'marsias', with the recitation of a *rubai*, which he rendered with such aplomb, that the audience always looked forward to hearing more and more of his *rubaies*. The success of Anees and Dabir in this field produced many emulators of their example who tended this verse form with special care and skill.

Among those who came after Anees and Dabir, and made a notable contribution to the enrichment of this genre should be mentioned Hali (1837-1914), Akbar Allahabadi (1846-1921), and Shad Azimabadi (1846-1927). *The rubaies* of Shad Azimabadi are devotional and didactic in their tone and content. In most of them, the poet is concerned with the predicament of man, problem of good and evil, transience of life, incorrigibility of human nature, and the grace and glory of God. But Shad is not paying a mere lip service to God and goodness—he speaks out of conviction which, aided by his artistic competence, results in impressive poetry.

Both Hali and Akbar used this form as a vehicle of social and religious reform, though both of them adopted widely different styles, which may even be called diametrically opposite. Hali, like Anees and Dabir before him, tenders his advice in the right earnest, like a pulpit preacher, without, however, ceasing to be a poet. Akbar, on the contrary, exploits to the full his weaponry of wit and humour to achieve his reformative goals. Akbar also had the boldness of using in his *rubaies* some popular English words and names so as to give a touch of sprightliness to his satire, and to reflect the new fashion of mixing English and Urdu in social conversation. Akbar thus made valuable innovations in the style of the *rubai* and gave it a touch of lightness which was absent from the compositions of his predecessors. Here is a specimen of Akbar's witticism:

پرانی روشنی میں اور نئی میں فرق اتنا ہے
اسے کشتی نہیں ملتی، اسے ساحل نہیں ملتا
کتاب دل مجھے کافی ہے اکبر درسِ حکمت کو
میں اسپنسر سے مستغنی ہوں مجھ سے مل نہیں ملتا

This is what differentiates cultures new and old,
One has no shore in sight, the other lacks the oar;
The book of heart, Akbar, contains the finest lore,
I take my cue from Spenser, Mill I ignore.

Hali's reformative zeal was not confined to social and religious sphere alone. If "Mussaddas-e-Hali", is inspired by moral and religious fervour, his prose treatise, "Mukaddama-e-Shair-o-Shairi" is an important critical document, in the tradition of Wordsworth's "Preface to the Lyrical Ballads", aimed at reforming Urdu poetry, particularly Urdu *ghazal*, which, in the hands of popular poetasters, was losing touch with the living language, and with the reality of emotional experience. In the following *rubai* Hali expresses his discontent with the conventional kinds of poets and poems:

بلبل کی چہن میں ہم زبانی چھوڑی
بزمِ شعرا میں شعرخوانی چھوڑی
جب سے دلِ زندہ تو نے ہم کو چھوڑا
ہم نے بھی تیری رام کہانی چھوڑی

Here I repudiate the songs of Nightingale,
No more shall I the poetic meets regale,
Since the day you quit me, O, my valiant heart,
I, too, have done with your oft-repeated tale.

Partly as a result of Hali's criticism, and partly due to the social and political changes occurring in the country after the First World War, Urdu poets were looking for new directions, and for a new poetic form which, retaining the lyricism of the *ghazal*, could also respond effectively to the more mundane needs of life—need for moral reform, material prosperity and political freedom. Some of the new poets of the early decades of the 20th century abdicated the *ghazal* in favour of the *nazm*; some, like Ahmed Nadim Qasimi and Noon Meem Rashid, opted for *nazm* in free-verse; while those who stuck, like Josh, Firaq and Hasrat Mohani, to the traditional form of the *ghazal*, preferred to invest it with the continuity of the *nazm*. The search for a poetic form that should be at once lyrical and functional, proved specially beneficial for the *rubai*, which, within its brief space of four lines can perform the twin tasks of singing and sermonising together. Moreover, the *rubai* was more suitable to meet the demand for "art for life's sake", which was gaining precedence over the aesthetic ideal of "art for art's sake". Consequently, the verse form of *rubai* was avidly seized and lovingly cultivated by several 20th century poets among whom Josh Malihabadi, Firaq

Gorakhpuri, and Amjad Hyderabadi, stand foremost.

Josh Malihabadi (1898-1982) is known as the poet of revolution and youth. Starting with the *ghazal*, he turned to the *nazm*, which, charged with the fire and fervour of partriotism, was instrumental in stirring the hearts of the Indian people who were then engaged in fighting the war of Independence. A famous quatrain with which Josh used to announce his poetic mission shows his characteristic manner:

سنو اے ساکنانِ بزمِ ہستی
ندا کیا آرہی ہے آسمان سے
آزادی کا اک لمحہ ہے بہتر
غلامی کی حیاتِ جاوداں سے

O, ye denizens of this earth,
Hark, what the heavens proclaim:
"A single moment freedom-crowned,
Outweighs eternal life in chains."

During his stay in Hyderabad Josh came in contact with Amjad Hyderabadi, another specialist of the *rubai* who, it seems, kindled Josh's instinctive aptitude for this form. Another poet who influenced Josh in this respect was Jagat Mohan Lal Rawan, who, like Josh, was a poetic disciple of Aziz Lucknavi. Josh wrote more than a thousand *rubaies* most of which can be found collected in his volume: *Janoon-o-Hikmat, Simoom-o-Saba,* and *Arsh-o-Farsh.* Though these rubaies deal with a variety of themes including politics, patriotism, philosophy, social reform, love, nature and romance, his favourite theme is wine and beauty, which makes him a poetical descendent of Omar Khayyam, the purveyor of the Epicurean philosophy of "Drink and be merry". This is how in the manner of the Persian poet, Josh sums up the meaning and purpose of life:

کل رات کو کیا جوشِ میں آیا ساقی
میرے شیون پہ گنگنایا ساقی
میں نے جو کہا مقصدِ ہستی کیا ہے
ساغر چھلکا کے مسکرایا ساقی

How flushed and thrilled was Saqi yesternight!
As I sat complaining, he hummed with delight;
When I asked in earnest: "What's the aim of life?"
He shook his flask in style, and gave a subtle smile.

Also in his admirable ability to create the effect of a dialogue within the parameters of the *rubai*, Josh reminds us of Khayyam. The following *rubai* shows his technical skill at its best:

یہ رات گئے عینِ طرب کے ہنگام
پرتو یہ پڑا پشت سے کس کا سرِ جام
یہ کون ہے؟ "جبریل ہوں" "کیوں آئے ہو"
"سرکارِ فلک کے نام کوئی پیغام!"

Late at night when I am ecstasy engrossed,
Whose reflection from behind in my cup is cast?
"Who art thou?" "Gabriel." "What brings you here?"
"Do you have, my Lord, a message for the gods?"

Firaq Gorakhpuri (1896-1982) owes his first *rubai* to a quarrel with Josh, his friend and contemporary. When on some trivial issue they fell out, Firaq voiced his angry protest in his maiden *rubai*:

معصوم خلوصِ باطن کچھ بھی نہیں
وہ قرب و قدرِ باہمی کچھ بھی نہیں
اک رات کی وہ جھڑپ، وہ جھک جھک پڑ
اور آٹھ برس کی دوستی کچھ بھی نہیں

That innocent attachment, all meaning has lost,
That closeness, that regard, matter not a jot,
That bark and bite of one night, that billingsgate is everything,
That friendship eight-year long is reduced to naught.

Reading this *rubai* alongside the *rubaies* of Dard, Anees, or Dabir, we can form an idea of the development in scope that this genre has seen over the years. A verse form that began on a devout and solemn note, as a means of moral edification or philosophical reflection, has taken within its sweep not only the topics of love, wine and women, but also, as exemplified above, the more mundane task of retort and repartee. This, however, is not the characteristic manner of Firaq whose best *rubaies*, collected in the volume entitled, *Roop,* may be described as vignettes of beauty—of sensuous female beauty, presented with the aid of fresh similes and imagery drawn from nature and fine arts, from music in particular:

لہروں میں کھلا کمل نہائے جیسے
دوشیزہ صبح گنگنائے جیسے
یہ روپ، یہ لوچ، یہ ترنم، یہ نکھار
بچہ سوتے میں مسکرائے جیسے

Like a blooming lotus water-steeped,
Like the maid of Morn, murmuring sweet,
Such beauty, such brightness, such melody, such grace,
Like a tender babe asmile in sleep.

Firaq's style possesses simplicity, sensuousness, and a poignant sweetness reminiscent of Mir Taqi Mir. Another distinction of Firaq lies in his attempt to reform the language of poetry. He has tried to bring Urdu language close to his native soil by purging it of heavy Persian diction and by incorporating into it indigenous, easy-to-understand words and images derived from Sanskrit or Hindi. In his Preface to *Roop* Firaq writes: "Urdu poetry should take full advantage of the poetry of Hindi and Sanskrit..... I have introduced into these *rubaies* a selection of words from Sanskrit, taking care that they do not damage the basic sweetness and flow of Urdu. All these *rubaies* are written in the tradition of 'Shringar Ras'. They have been given a leaven of Hindi culture, yet they are rooted in the eternal verities of life." Some critics* have found fault with Firaq's habit of yoking together Hindi and Urdu, which, they complain, militates against the basic spirit and culture of the Urdu language and makes it look awkward and obscure. Such criticism is not justified. If a reader can understand the allusion to Yousaf and Zuleikha, or appreciate the metaphor of rose and nightingale, he can as well understand the nearer-at-home allusion to Krishna and Radha, or the metaphor of the "Chand" and "Chakore". Firaq's attempt to simplify the language of Urdu poetry by drawing it closer to the language of the soil, is in keeping with Wordsworth's advice that the language of poetry should be a "selection of language really used by men". Firaq's example, one feels, deserves appreciation and emulation.

The third major poet of the *rubai* to whom goes the credit, along with Josh and Firaq, of perfecting and popularising this form in the 20th century is Amjad Hyderabadi. Amjad is exclusively a poet of the *rubai*, unlike Firaq or Josh, both of whom are as deeply interested in the *nazm* and *ghazal* as in the *rubai*. Amjad's *rubaies* are deeply devotional, mystical, or ethical, falling, as such, in the tradition of Dard, Anees and Dabir. He is often called the Sarmad of Urdu poetry. Yet he could not attain the popularity which fell to the share of Firaq and Josh. Notwithstanding their technical

---

* See Firman Fatehpuri, *Urdu Rubai*, Modern Publishers, Karachi, 1962, pp. 94, 97.

perfection and solemnity of thought, his *rubaies* lack the defiant liveliness of Josh, or the rich sensuousness of Firaq. But this is not to deny Amjad's claim to be considered as a master-poet, who not only practised, but also propagated the art of the *rubai*.

Quite a few other important poets of the 20th century successfully tried their hand at the *rubai*. Among these may be mentioned Aasi Ghazipuri, Shad Azimabadi, Jagat Mohan Lal Rawan, Fani Badayuni, Yagana Changezi, Tilok Chand Mehroom, and Naresh Kumar Shad. I'll not dwell on the individual merits of these poets. Selections from their works included in the following pages will amply illustrate the quality and calibre of their mind and art. The fact that the *rubai* has drawn so many talented poets into its fold speaks volumes for its inherent strength and richness. As already noted, the *rubai* combines in its texture the advantages both of subjective and objective poetry. If it can embody the poet's observations about life and death, nature, politics, religion or morality, it can also express, in an apt, artistic way, the emotional and psychological moods of the poet, and give a lyrical treatment to the all-important themes of love and beauty. At the same time, the *rubai* is the shortest complete poem in Urdu, next only, in brevity, to the Japanese *Haiku*, a poem of seventeen syllables, containing three lines; and to the Hindi *Doha*, a self-sufficient couplet. In the present age of high speed and hectic haste when people are discarding the old practice of letter-writing in favour of phone calls, when short story is getting preference over the novel, *rubai*, which admits of no verbiage, no superfluities, and is both musical and meaningful, stands a good chance of development and growth.

URDU RUBAIYAT

مِرزا مُحمّد رفیع سَودا

جہاں کے بحر میں اے دل لباس اِتنا چاہ
کہ جوں حباب وہی پیرہن وہی ہو کلاہ
تو کس تلاش میں سر مارتا پھرے ہے؟ عُمر
برنگِ رشتۂ سوزن ہے ہر قدم کوتاہ

تِرا دل مجھ سے نہیں ملتا میرا جی رہ نہیں سکتا
غرض ایسی مُصیبت ہے کہ میں کچھ کہہ نہیں سکتا
ترے آگے میری آنکھوں سے آنسو کیونکہ چلتے ہیں
جو تُو دریا سے گذرے ہے تو پانی بہہ نہیں سکتا

اگر دُنیا میں اب یوں ہی سجن رسمِ وفا ہوگا
تو کس اُمّید پر کوئی کسی سے آشنا ہوگا
جو یہ منظور ہے تم کو مرا دل لے کے جی لینا
گیا ایک مجھ سا دنیا سے ترے صدقے تو کیا ہوگا

MIRZA MOHAMMED RAFI SAUDA
(1713-1781)

In the sea of life, O heart, be thou sparsely dressed,
Bubble-like, one only sheet should form your cloak and crest,
What is it you are fretting for, why this hectic haste?
Life, like the needle's thread, diminishes at every step.

Jahaan ke bahr mein, ai dil, libaas itna chaah,
Ke joon habaab wohi parahan, wohi ho kulah;
Tu kis talaash mein sar maarta phire hai? umr
Barang-e-rishta-e-sozan hai har qadam kotaah.

Your heart doesn't accord with mine, I, without you, restless feel,
In what a fix I'm caught, I can't reveal;
How can my tears, in your presence, ever dare to flow?
When you pass beside the river, water stands congealed.

Tera dil mujh se nahin milta, mera ji rah nahin sakta,
Gharz aisi maseebat hai ke main kuchh kah nahin sakta;
Tere aage meri aankhon se aansu kyonke chalte hain,
Jo tu darya se guzre hai, tau paani bah nahin sakta.

If such be the fate of love in this world, O, friend,
Why should then anyone anyone befriend?
If you want to steal my heart and live unconcerned,
What would happen if for you someone his life may end?

Agar duniya mein ab yunhi sajan rasam-e-wafa hoga,
Tau kis umeed par koi kisi se Aashna hoga,
Jo yeh manzur hai tum ko mera dil le ke ji lena,
Gaya yak mujh saa duniya se tere sadqe to kya hoga?

سودا

بوؤں میں تخمِ گل کو جہاں واں زقُوم ہو
پالوں جو عندلیب قفس میں تو بُوم ہو
اپنے چمن کو فائدہ کیا تجھ سے اے صبا
یہ جا ہے وہ کہ یاں دمِ عیسیٰ سموم ہو

گدا دستِ اہلِ کرم دیکھتے ہیں
ہم اپنا ہی دم اور قدم دیکھتے ہیں
غرض کفر سے کچھ، نہ دیں سے ہے مطلب
تماشائے دیر و حرم دیکھتے ہیں

ساقی گئی بہار، رہی دل میں یہ ہوس
تو منّتوں سے جام دے اور میں کہوں کہ بس
کچھ اس چمن میں آ کے نہ دکھلائیں جوں حباب
آبِ رواں کو سیر کیا سو بھی یک نفس

Sauda

If I sow the seeds of flowers, nettles only grow,
A nightingale by me encaged becomes an owl, I trow;
What good to my garden can you cause, O breeze?
Scorching like the Simoom here the breath of Christ doth blow.

Boun main tukham-e-gul ko jahaan waan zaqoom ho,
Paalun jo andlib qafas mein tau boom ho,
Apne chaman ko faida kya tujh se ai saba,
Yeh jaa hai woh ke yaan dam-e-Isah simoom ho.

At the donors' hand the beggars gaze,
Our own strength and steps we gauge,
Faith or heresy concern us not,
Shrines and mosques our sight engage.

Gada dast-e-ahl-e-karam dekhte hain,
Hum apna hi dam aur qadam dekhte hain,
Gharz kufar se kuchh, na deen se hai matlab,
Tamashaa-e-der-o-haram dekhte hain.

My longing lingers still, vanished though is spring,
I should say, "No more," when Saqi pours the drink;
Nothing in the garden did I really see; a fleeting while,
Bubble-like, I glimpse the stream and sink.

Saqi, gai bahaar, rahi dil mein yeh hawas,
Tu mannaton se jaam de aur main kahun, ke bas,
Kuchh is chaman mein aa ke na dekha main joon habab,
Aab-e-rawaan ko sair kiya, so bhi yak nafus.

سودا

ساقی ہماری توبہ تجھ پر ہے کیوں گوارا
مِنّت نہیں تو ظالم ترغیب یا اشارا
یک بار ہی چھکا دے ساقی کہ فصلِ گُل کو
عرصہ کہاں ہے اِتنا دے جام تُو دوبارہ

مُجھ کو نہیں ہے دِل میں ترے راہ کیا کروں
پَر بے اثر ہے عِشق مِرا ، آہ کیا کروں
سُن کر ہزار شکل مِرا حال یُوں کہا
تُو تو کسی طرح نہیں دِل نخواہ کیا کروں

سودا قمارِ عشق میں شیریں سے کوہکن
بازی اگرچہ پا نہ سکا سَر تو کھو سکا
کس مُنہ سے پھر تُو آپ کو کہتا ہے عِشق باز
اَے رُوسیاہ ، تجھ سے تو یہ بھی نہ ہو سکا

Sauda

My excuse of abstinence, Saqi, you should just ignore,
Persuade or prompt, O cruel, if you can't implore;
Surfeit me all at once, spring is on the wing,
For the second round of drink, it can wait no more.

Saqi, hamari tauba tujh par hai kyon gawaraa,
Mannat nahin to zaalim targhib yaa isharaa,
Yak baar hi chhaka de Saqi ke fasal-e-gul ko,
Arsa kahaan hai itna de jaam tu do barah.

I cannot reach up to your heart, what am I to do?
Ineffective is my love, alas, what am I to do?
Hearing my case in thousand shapes, thus did he
     pronounce:
"In no way are you likeable, tell me, what to do."

Mujh ko nahin hai dil mein tere raah, kya karun?
Par, be-asar hai ishq mera, aah, kya karun!
Sun kar hazaar shakal mera haal yoon kaha:
"Tu tau kisi tarah nahin dil khwah, kya karun!"

If Kohkan couldn't win the prize of Shirin's love,
He at least didn't demur, but laid down his head;
How can you call yourself a lover, do you have the cheek?
When, Sauda, O brazen-face, you didn't even drop down
     dead!

Sauda, qamaar-e-ishq mein Shirin se Kohkan,
Baazi agarcheh paa na saka, sar tau kho saka;
Kis munh se phir tu aap ko kahta hai ishq baaz,
Ai roo-siaah, tujh se tau ye bhi na ho saka.

خواجہ میر درؔد

کب، جس کو ہو دُنیا کی طلب ہے، بیٹھ سکے
جِس دل میں ہوس بھری ہو، کب بیٹھ سکے
تسکین، شہودِ حق سے ہوتی ہے نصیب
اُٹھ جاتے نظر سے خَلق، تب بیٹھ سکے

پَیدا کرے ہر چند تقدّس بندا
مُشکل ہے کہ حِرص سے ہو دل بر کندا
جنّت میں بھی اکل و شرب سے نہیں ہے نجات
دوزخ کا، بہشت میں بھی ہو گا دَھندا

یہ راہِ خاک ساری میں سَیر سے قطعے کی ہے
نقشِ جبیں ہے میرا، ہر نقشِ پا جہاں ہے
مت موت کی تمنّا اے درد ہر گھڑی کر
دُنیا کو دیکھ تُو بھی، تُو تو ابھی جواں ہے

KHWAJA MIR DARD
(1720-1784)

Can a man of mundane aims ever sit at rest?
Lust-infected heart with peace is never blest,
If you want calm content, seek the Truth divine,
When you rise above the world, you settle down to rest.

Kab, jis ko ho duniya ki talab, beth sake,
Jis dil mein hawas bhari ho, kab beth sake,
Taskin shahud-e-haq se hoti hai naseeb,
Uth jaae nazr se khalaq, tab beth sake.

Let a man try his best to cleanse and purify,
Never can he purge his heart of the lusts of life,
No escape from sensuous feast even in Paradise,
Even the holy Heaven paths of hell provides.

Paida kare har chand taqaddas bandaa,
Mushkil hai ke hirs se ho dil barkanda,
Jannat mein bhi akal-o-sharab se nahin hai nijaat,
Dozakh ka, bahisht mein bhi hoga dhanda.

I have measured with my brow this road from end to end,
Where I saw Thy foot-print, there my brow did bend;
Let not the death-wish, Dard, thus obsess your mind,
Time for you to see the world, you are young, my friend.

Yeh raah-e-khaak saari main sar se qata ki hai,
Naqsh-e-jabeen hai mera, har naqsh-e-paa jahaan hai,
Mat maut ki tamanna, ai Dard, har ghari kar,
Duniya ko dekh tu bhi, tu tau abhi jawan hai.

دَرد

کُچھ آپ ہی گِرا کے ، آپ ہی کُچھ چُنتا ہے
کہتا کُچھ آپی ، آپ ہی کُچھ سُنتا ہے
اے دَرد ! ہمیشہ یہ دِلِ دِیوانہ
کیا کیا کُچھ اُدھیڑتا ہے اور بُنتا ہے

ہم نے بھی کبھُو جام و سُبو دیکھا تھا
جو کُچھ کہ نہیں ہے رُو بَرُو دیکھا تھا
اُن باتوں کو اَب جو غور کرے اے دَرد
کُچھ خواب سا تھا کہ وہ کبھُو دیکھا تھا

غم کھاتے ہیں اور آنسو نِت پیتے ہیں
دِن رات ہمیں عجب طرح بِیتے ہیں
گُذرے ہے جو کُچھ کہ گُذرے ہے ، کیا کہیّے
پر ، تحفگی یہ کہ اَب تلک جیتے ہیں

Dard

Dropping something down, it picks it on its own,
Itself it speaks, responds on its own,
This silly heart, O Dard, is always engaged,
In stitching and unstitching, all on its own.

Kuchh aapi gira ke, aapi kuchh chunta hai,
Kahta kuchh aapi, aapi kuchh sunta hai,
Ai Dard! hamesha yeh dil-e-diwana,
Kya kya kuchh udherta hai aur bunta hai.

We too had once tasted the joys of cup and flask,
What we only crave for, we once had drunk that draught;
When we think of such things now, Dard, they merely
      seem,
Vague, empty dreams, buried in the past.

Hum ne bhi kabhu jaam-o-saboo dekha tha,
Jo kuchh ke nahin hai roo-ba-roo dekha tha,
Un baaton ko ab jo ghaur kare ai Dard,
Kuchh khwaab tha ke woh kabhu dekha tha.

We drink our tears, on sorrows we survive,
In a strange style we spend our life;
What all we go through, we can't describe,
How very surprising, we are still alive!

Ghum khaate hain aur aansu nit peete hain,
Din raat hamen ajab tarah beete hain,
Guzre hai jo kuchh ke guzre hai, kya kahiye,
Par, tuhfgi yeh ke ab talak jeete hain.

درؔد

کس کا ہے کون، کیا کسُو سے کہنا
اپنا اپنا ہر ایک کا ہے لَہنا
گذرے ہے اب اس طرح سے اپنی اے درؔد
رونا چُھپکے پڑے، اکیلے رَہنا

زُلف کھاتی ہے بَل اُدھر اُس کی
دل اِدھر پیچ و تابؔ کرتا ہے
مَیں تو کہتا ہوں بات پردے کی
کیوں تو اِتنا اِحجابؔ کرتا ئے

پیسری چلی اَور گئی جوانی اپنی
اے درد کہاں ہے زِندگانی اپنی
کل اور کوئی بیاں کرے گا اِس کو
کہتے ہیں اب آپ کہانی اپنی

Dard

Whom can you call your own, of whom complain?
Self-centred is every one, chasing selfish aim,
This is how our life goes, nowadays, O Dard!
We lie weeping in silence, and loneliness amain!

Kis ka hai kaun kya kasu se kahna,
Apna apna har ek ka hai lehna,
Guzre hai ab is tarah se apni ai Dard,
Rona chupke pare, akele rahna.

There your tresses twist and turn,
Here my heart is deeply churned;
I speak in confidence, betwixt us two,
Why you with coyness blush and burn?

Zulf khaati hai bal udhar us ki,
Dil idhar pech-o-taab karta hai,
Main to kahta hun baat parde ki,
Kyon tu itna hijaab karta hai?

Youth is gone past, age is slipping away,
Where to find, O Dard, those distant, bygone days?
Lips of others will recount tomorrow
The tale we ourselves tell today.

Peeri chali aur gai jawani apni,
Ai Dard, kahaan hai zindgaani apni,
Kal aur koi bayaan karega is ko,
Kahte hain ab aap kahaani apni.

میر تقی میر

جِن جِن کو تھا یہ عشق کا آزار مر گئے
اکثر ہمارے ساتھ کے بیمار مر گئے
صد کاروانِ وفا ہے کوئی پوچھتا نہیں
گویا متاعِ دل کے خریدار مر گئے

اِک شخص مجھی سا تھا کہ تھا مجھ سے پہ عاشق
وہ اُس کی وفا پیشگی وہ اُس کی جوانی
یہ کہہ کے جو رویا تو لگا کہنے نہ کہہ میر
سُنتا نہیں میں ظلم رسیدوں کی کہانی

کاہے کوئی خرابؔ و خواری ہوتا
کاہے کو کسی پہ جان بھاری ہوتا
دِل خواہ ملاپ ہوتا تو مِلتے
اے کاش کہ عشق اختیاری ہوتا

36

MIR TAQI MIR
(1722-1808)

All who suffered the ague of love have since expired,
Most of my fellow-patients have to their graves retired,
Caravans freighted with faith hawk about in vain,
It seems in the world at large, the heart has no buyer.

Jin jin ko tha yeh ishq kaa aazaar mar gaye,
Aksar hamaare saath ke bimaar mar gaye;
Sad carwaan-e-wafa hai koi puchhta nahin,
Goya mitaa-e-dil ke kharidaar mar gaye.

"It was a man like me, who loved someone like you,
"Oh, his fidelity, his youth winged with hope!"
When at this I broke down, I was brusquely told:
"Stop it Mir, I shall not hear about the oppressed folk."

"Ik shakhs mujhi saa tha, ke tha tujh se pe aashiq,
"Woh uski wafa-peshgi, woh uski jawaani!"
Yeh keh ke jo roya to laga kahne na keh Mir,
Sunta nahin main zulm raseedon ki kahaani.

Why should I undergo humiliation untold?
Or, hang heavily on someone else's soul?
I would welcome a meeting if heartily wished,
Would that love were something under our control!

Kaahe koi kharaab-o-khwari hotaa,
Kaahe ko kisi par jaan bhaari hotaa,
Dil khwah milaap hotaa tau milte,
Ai kaash ke ishq akhtiari hotaa.

میر

مصائب اور تھے پر دِل کا جانا
عجب اِک سانحہ سا ہوگیا ہے
سرہانے میرؔ کے کوئی نہ بولو
ابھی ٹک روتے روتے سوگیا ہے

ہر لحظہ جلاتا ہے کڑھاتا ہے مجھے
ہر آن ستاتا ہے کھپاتا ہے مجھے
کل میں نے جو کہا، رنج سے حاصل میرے
بولا تیرا آزار خوش آتا ہے مجھے

کچھ موجِ ہوا پیچاں اے میرؔ نظر آئی
شاید کہ بہار آئی، زنجیر نظر آئی
دِلّی کے نہ تھے کوچے اوراقِ مصوّر تھے
جو شکل نظر آئی تصویر نظر آئی

38

Mir

Many a trouble have I borne, but the passing of my heart
Is a traumatic event, rather strange and deep;
Pray, gently speak beside the bed of Mir,
Sobbing for hours he's just gone to sleep.

Musaaib aur the par dil ka jaanaa,
Ajab ik saaniha saa ho gaya hai,
Sarhaane Mir ke aahista bolo,
Abhi tuk rote rote so gaya hai.

All the time he teases me and doth torment,
Annoys and irritates without a cause or end,
When I ask, why dost thou torture me in vain?
"It gives me pleasure," he says, "to cause you discontent."

Har lahza jalaata hai, kurhaata hai mujhe,
Har aan sataata hai, khapaata hai mujhe,
Kal main ne jo kaha ranj se haasil mere,
Bola, tera aazaar khush aata hai mujhe.

I have sighted, Mir, some swirling whiffs of breeze,
Perhaps the spring arrives, the chain beckons to me,
Winsome were the streets of Delhi, like a work of art,
Every figure that I met was a master-piece.

Kuchh mauj-e-hawa pechaan, ai Mir nazr aai,
Shaaid ke bahaar aai, zanjeer nazr aai,
Dilli ke na the kuche, auraaq-e-musawwar the,
Jo shakal nazr aai, tasveer nazr aai.

میر

میر آوارۂ عالم جو سُنا ہے تو ہے
خاک آلودہ وُہ اے بادِ صبا ایں ہی ہوں
کاسۂ سر کو لیے مانگتا دیدار پھرے
سیر وہ جان سے، بیزار گدا ایں ہی ہوں

مُغاں! مُجھ مَست بِن خندۂ ساغر نہ ہووے گا
مئے گلگوں کا شیشہ ہچکیاں لے لے کے رووے گا
کیا ہے خوں مِرا پامال یہ سُرخی نہ چھوٹے گی
اگر قاتل تو اپنے پاؤں سو پانی سے دھووے گا

کچھ تمھیں مِلنے سے بیزار ہو میرے، ورنہ
دوستی تنگ نہیں، عیب نہیں، عار نہیں
ناز و انداز و ادا، عشوہ و اغماض وحَیَ
آبِ گل میں تری سب کچھ ہے مگر پیار نہیں

Mir

Mir, who is also called the wanderer of the world,
That dust-besplattered being, O, breeze, is none else but me;
Carrying the bowl of his head, begging the favour of a glimpse,
Weary of life, a beggar distressed, is none else but me.

Mir aawaara-e-aalam jo suna hai tu ne,
Khaak aaluda woh, ai baad-e-sabaa main hi hoon,
Kaasa-e-sar ko liye mangtaa deedaar phire,
Seer woh jaan se, bezaar gada main hi hoon.

Without me, O tavern-keeper, the cups will cease to laugh,
Sobbing, hiccuping all the time will lie the purple flask,
Now that you have shed my blood, these gules will not go,
O, assassin, even if your feet you wash and wash.

Mughaan mujh mast bin khanda-e-saaghar na hovegaa
Mai-e-gulgun ka sheesha hichkian le le ke rovegaa;
Kiya hai khun mera paamaal, yeh surkhi na chhutegi,
Agar qatil tu apne paaon sau paani se dhovegaa.

You alone are sick of me, in the world, otherwise,
Friendship is no cause for shame, no crime, no vice;
Airs, graces, glances, coyness, coquetry, and guile,
You possess everything except love, the crown of life.

Kuchh tumhin milne se bezaar ho mere warna,
Dosti nang nahin, aib nahin, aar nahin,
Naaz-o-andaaz-o-ada, ushwa-o-aghmaaz-o-haya,
Aab-o-gil mein teri sab kuchh hai magar pyaar nahin.

میر

جھمکی دِکھا کے طُور کو جن نے جلا دیا
آئی قیامت اُن سے جو پَردہ اُٹھا دیا
اب بھی دماغِ رفتہ ہمارا ہے عَرش پر
گو آسماں نے خاک میں ہم کو مِلا دیا

دِل فرطِ اضطراب سے سیماب سا ہُوا
چہرہ تمام زرد زرِ نابُ سا ہُوا
سمجھے تھے ہم تو میر کو عاشق اُسی گھڑی
جب نام تیرا سُن کے وہ بیتاب سا ہُوا

ناگاہ جس کو عشق کا آزار ہو گیا
سہل آگے اُس کے مُردن دشوار ہو گیا
ہے حُسن کیا متاع کہ جس کو نظر پڑی
وہ جان بیچ کر بھی خریدار ہو گیا

Mir

He whose one glimpse can set the Mount ablaze,
Would bring the doom on earth, if he but unveils,
Our head, crazed and lost, still heavenward soars,
Though the mighty heaven to dust o'r pride has razed.

Jhamki dikha ke Tur ko jin ne jala diya,
Aai qayamat un ne jo parda utha diya;
Ab bhi dimagh-e-rafta hamara hai arsh par,
Go aasmaan ne khaak mein hum ko mila diya.

Quick-silver like quivers the heart by restlessness assailed,
The face, like pallid gold, has utterly paled;
We could at once see that Mir was in love,
When, hearing your name, he winced and quailed.

Dil fart-e-iztraab se seemaab saa hua,
Chehra tamaam zard zar-e-naab saa hua,
Samjhe the hum tau Mir ko aashiq usi ghari,
Jab naam tera sun ke woh betaab saa hua.

He whom the plague of love infects,
No fear of death his soul reflects,
There must be something in Beauty, for whosoever espies,
Readily stakes his life to own this rare asset.

Naagah jis ko ishq ka aazaar ho gaya,
Sahal aage uske murdan-e-dushwaar ho gaya,
Hai husn kya mitaa ke jisko nazr pari,
Woh jaan bech kar bhi kharidaar ho gaya.

میرؔ

ساکنِ دیر و حرم دونوں تلاشی ہیں ترے
تو خدا جانے کہاں ہے کیونکے تجھ کو پائیے
دُور ہی سے ہوش کھو دیتی ہے اُس کی بُوئے خوش
آپ میں رہیئے تو اُس کے پاس بھی تک جائیے

لوگ بہت پوچھا کرتے ہیں، کیا کہئے میاں کیا ہے عشق
کچھ کہتے ہیں سرِّ الٰہی، کچھ کہتے ہیں خدا ہے عشق
اُلفت سے پرہیز کیا کر، کُلفت اِس میں نہایت ہے
یعنی درد و رنج و تعب ہے، آفتِ جان و بلا ہے عشق

ہم کو کہنے کے تیئں بزم میں جا دیتے ہیں
بیٹھنے پاتے نہیں ہیں کہ اُٹھا دیتے ہیں
اُس شہِ حسن کا اِقبال کہ ظالم کے تیئں
ہر طرف سینکڑوں درویش دُعا دیتے ہیں

Mir

Dwellers of the mosque and shrine both are on your quest,
God knows where you are, how to find you best!
Thy scent defrauds our sense even from afar,
We must first recover ourselves, ere we seek Thy nest.

Saakan-e-der-o-haram donon talaashi hain tere,
Tu khuda jaane kahaan hai kyonke tujh ko paaiye,
Dur se hi hosh kho deti hai uski bu-e-khush,
Aap mein rahye tau us ke pass bhi tuk jaaiye.

Often do the people ask, what's love? Who can explain?
Some call it the fount divine, by some 'tis God proclaimed,
You should beware of love, it causes endless pain,
Sorrow, suffering, terror, torture—love is known by many a name.

Log bahut puchha karte hain, kya kahiye miyaan kya hai ishq,
Kuchh kahte hain sarr-e-Ilaahi, kuchh Kahte hain khuda hai ishq,
Ulfat se parhez kiya kar, kulfat ismein nihaait hai,
Yaani dard-o-ranj-o-taab hai, aafat-e-jaan hai, balaa hai ishq.

We are asked to take a seat for mere formality sake,
Even before we manage to sit, we hear the word, "vacate";
How privileged is that dear despot that in every place,
Many a saint blesses his name, for him invokes His grace.

Hum ko kahne ke taeen bazm mein jaa dete hain,
Bethne paate nahin hain ke utha dete hain,
Us shah-e-husn ka iqbal ke zaalim ke taeen,
Har taraf sainkron darvesh dua dete hain.

میر

دلِ دل دل لوگ کہا کرتے ہیں تم نے جانا کیا ہے دل
چشمِ بصیرت وا ہو وے تو عجائب دید کی جا ہے دل
اوجِ و موج کا آشوب اُسکے لیکے زمیں سی فلک تک ہے
صورت میں تو قطرۂ خوں ہے معنی میں دریا ہے دل

ہر صبح غموں میں شام کی ہے میں نے
خونابہ کشی مدام کی ہے میں نے
یہ مہلتِ کم کہ جس کو کہتے ہیں عمر
مر مر کے غرض تمام کی ہے میں نے

مسجد میں تو شیخ کو خروشاں دیکھا
میخانے میں شورِ بادہ نوشاں دیکھا
اِک گوشۂ عافیت جہاں میں ہم نے
دیکھا تو محلّۂ خموشاں دیکھا

Mir

Everywhere they talk of heart, do you know what heart may be?
For those with discerning eyes the heart presents a sight to see;
The tumult of its rising tides fills the space of earth and skies,
Apparently a drop of blood, the heart conceals a mighty sea.

Dil dil log kaha karte hain tum ne jaanaa kya hai dil,
Chashm-e-baseerat waa hove to ajaaib deed ki jaa hai dil;
Auj-o-mauj ka aashob uske le ke zamin se falak tak hai,
Surat mein to qatra-e-khun hai, maani mein darya hai dil.

I have moved from morn to night plunged in sorrows' flood,
Every day in place of wine I have drunk my blood,
This brief respite, by men called life,
A bitter struggle I had to wage to tide over this flood.

Har subah ghamon mein shaam ki hai main ne,
Khunaba kashi madaam ki hai main ne,
Yeh muhlat-e-kam ke jisko kahte hain umr,
Mar mar ke gharz tamaam ki hai main ne.

The mosque was found astir with the priestly roar,
The tavern reverberated with the drinkers 'encores';
In vain I sought a peaceful nook on this noisy shore,
Only in the grave-yard I had my peace restored.

Masjid mein to sheikh ko kharoshaan dekha,
Mai khane mein shor-e-baada noshaan dekha,
Ik gosha-e-aafeeat jahaan mein hum ne,
Dekha to mahalla-e-khamoshaan dekha.

میر

مِلیئے اُس شخص سے جو آدم ہووے
ناز اُس کو کمال پر بہت کم ہووے
ہو گرمِ سخن تو گرد آوے یک خلق
خاموش رہے تو ایک عالَم ہووے

دِلّی میں بہت سخت کی اب کی گزران
دل کو کر سنگ
غیرت نہ رہی عاقبت کار نہ شان
کھینچا یہ ننگ
یاروں میں نہ تھا کوئی مروّت جو کرے
اُجڑے تھے گھر
تا حدِّ نظر صاف پڑے تھے میدان
عرصہ تھا تنگ

48

Mir

A man who is truly human, let us love and seek,
Despite his mighty talent, such a man is meek;
The world flocks around him when he doth discourse,
He's a world in himself, when silence he doth keep.

Miliye us shakhs se jo aadam hove,
Naaz usko kamaal par bahut kam hove;
Ho garm-e-sakhun to gird aawe yak khalaq,
Khamosh rahe to ek aalam hove.

A hard time I spent in Delhi—stiffening my heart to stone,
No honour, no grace, no glory—ignominy untoned;
I did not have a friend to counsel or console—desolate every home;
Barren wastes stared in the face, I felt benumbed—weary and forlorn.

Dilli mein bahut sakht ki ab ke guzraan—dil ko kar sung,
Ghairat na rahi aaqbat kaar na shaan—khencha yeh nung;
Yaaron mein na tha koi murawat jo kare,—ujre the ghar,
Taa hadd-e-nazr saaf pare the maidaan—arsa tha tung.

قلندربخش جُرأت

کل واقف کار اپنے سے کہتا تھا وُہ یہ بات
جُرأت کے گھر رات کو مہمان گئے ہم
کیا جانیے کم بخت نے کیا ہم یہ کیا سِحر
جو بات نہ تھی ماننے کی مان گئے ہم

دیکھا جو اُس نے میرے جی کا کھونا
اور کھینچ کے آہِ سرد ہر دم رونا
مُنہ پھیر کے مُسکرا کے چُپکے سے کہا
آسان نہیں کِسی پہ عاشق ہونا

کچھ عشق میں تو مزہ نہ پایا ہم نے
اِس دل ہی کو مفت گنوایا ہم نے
اور جس کے لیے گنوایا دل کو جُرأت
اُس کو اپنا کبھی نہ پایا ہم نے

QALANDAR BAKHSH JURRAT
(1748-1809)

Yesterday he was telling this to someone one whom he knew,
"I was visiting Jurrat's place, one night, as it turned,
"What strange spell, I know not, that rogue on me did cast,
"I assented to the very thing, I should have spurned."

Kal waaqif kaar apne se kahta tha woh yeh baat,
Jurrat ke ghar raat ko mehmaan gaye hum,
Kya jaaneye kambakht ne kya hum pe kiya sihar,
Jo baat na thi maan-ne ki maan gaye hum.

When he saw how I bewailed my broken heart,
How deep I sighed, sans pause or stop,
Turning away his face, smilingly he quipped:
"To fall in love with someone is not an easy task!"

Dekha jo us ne mere ji ka khona,
Aur kheinch ke aah-e-sard, har dum rona,
Muhn pher ke, muskra ke, chupke se kaha,
"Aasaan nahin kisi par aashiq hona."

No joy to me did love impart,
In vain I lost my precious heart,
And he for whom my heart was lost,
Could not be owned at any cost.

Kuchh ishq mein to maza na paaya hum ne,
Is dil hi ko muft ganwaaya hum ne,
Aur jis ke lieye ganwaaya dil ko Jurrat,
Usko apna kabhi na paaya hum ne.

بہادر شاہ ظفر

کِتنے ہی بن کے شہر کے اور گاؤں کے نِشان
یُوں مِٹ گئے زمیں پہ کہ یُوں پاؤں کہ نِشان
گر نَخلِ خُشک کوئی کہیں رَہ گیا ظفر
پائے نہ اُس کے پاؤں تلے چھاؤں کے نِشان

کہاں وُہ مَہ جبیں اور ہم، کہاں وُہ وصل کی راتیں
مگر ہم نے کبھی تھا ایک یہ بھی خواب سا دیکھا
ظفر کی سَیرِ اِس گُلشن میں ہم نے پُر کسی گُل میں
نہ کچھ اُلفت کی بُو پائی، نہ کچھ رنگِ وفا دیکھا

سوزشِ دِل کو یُہں کیا خاک بُجھاتے میری
مُجھ کو رُسوائے جہاں دیدہ تَر کرتے ہیں
آتشِ عشق سے اُڑ جائیں سمندر کے حواس
یہ یہیں ہیں کہ جو اِس آگ میں گھر کرتے ہیں

BAHADUR SHAH ZAFAR
(1775-1869)

Many a mark of town and village, many a mark of waste,
Have faded like the foot-prints from the earth's face,
If at all a withered trunk, somewhere you espy,
In vain you may look beneath for a trace of shade.

Kitne hi ban ke shahr ke aur gaon ke nishaan,
Yoon mit gaye zameen pe ke yoon paon ke nishaan,
Gar nakhal-e-khushk koi kahin rah gaya, Zafar,
Paae na uske paaon tale chhaaon ke nishaan.

Whither I, whither my moon, and whither those nights of love?
But to see such a dream had once been my fate;
Although, Zafar, I combed the garden, I didn't see one bloom,
Breathing scent of love, reflecting hues of faith.

Kahan woh maha jabeen aur hum, kahan woh wasal ki raaten,
Magar hum ne kabhi tha ek yeh bhi khwaab saa dekha,
Zafar, ki sair is gulshan mein hum ne par kisi gul mein,
Na kuchh ulfat ki boo paai, na kuchh rang-e-wafa dekha

My streaming eyes can only bring public disgrace,
Impotent are they to quench internal fire;
With the heat of love, oceans vaporize,
I alone can bide in the heart of fire.

Sozish-e-dil ko hain kya khaak bujhaate meri,
Mujh ko ruswaa-e-jahan deeda-e-tar karte hain,
Aatish-e-ishq se ur jaaen samunder ke hawaas,
Yeh hameen hain ke jo is aag mein ghar karte hain.

ظفر

اِتنا نہ اپنے جامے سے باہر نکل کے چل
دُنیا ہے چل چلاؤ کا رستہ سنبھل کے چل
کیا چل سکے گا ہم سے کہ پہچانتے ہیں ہم
تو لاکھ اپنی چال کو، ظالم، بدل کے چل

آئے تم اِس دم کو جس دم آ گیا آنکھوں میں دم
میں نے دیکھا بھی نہ تم کو، میری جاں، اچھی طرح
اِتنی بھی فرصت نہ دی ہم کو فلک نے، اے ظفر
کرتے ہم اِس کوچے میں آہ و فغاں اچھی طرح

دِل ہے وُہی پسند جو تجھ پر فِدار ہے
جاں ہے وہی عزیز جو تجھ پر نثار ہو
ہُوں خاکِ راہ اُس کا، پر ایسا نہ ہو ظفر
میرا غبار خاطرِ نازک پہ بار ہو

Zafar

Don't outstrip your limits, keep thy self-control,
In this ever-shifting world, warily should you stroll;
You can't outsmart us, we know you through and through,
You may change and change your gait, you can't change your goal.

Itna na apne jaame se baahar nikal ke chal,
Duniya hai chal chalaao ka rasta sambhal ke chal;
Kya chal sakega hum se ke pahchaante hain hum,
Tu laakh apni chaal ko zaalim badal ke chal.

You arrived when I'd well-nigh breathed my last,
I couldn't even gaze at you, or please my heart;
I wasn't allowed to cry at length in this terrestrial lane,
The lease of life given to me was, indeed, too short.

Aae tum is dum ke jis dum aa gaya aankhon mein dum,
Main ne dekha bhi na tum ko meri jaan achhi tarah,
Itni bhi fursat na di hum ko falak ne, ai Zafar,
Karte is kuche mein hum aah-o-fughaan achhi tarah.

That heart alone is dear which delights in you,
That life is dearly prized which is pledged to you,
Albeit I'm the way-side dust, but, Zafar, I fear,
Lest this dust too heavily lies on that delicate shrew.

Dil hai wohi pasand jo tujh pe fida rahe,
Jaan hai wohi aziz jo tujh par nisaar ho,
Hun khaak-e-raah uska, par aisa na ho Zafar,
Mera gubaar khaatir-e-naazuk pe baar ho.

شیخ مُحمّد اِبراہیم ذوؔق

دُنیا کے عالم ذوؔق اُٹھا جائیں گے
ہم کیا کہیں کیا آئے تھے کیا جائیں گے
جب آئے تھے ہم روتے ہوئے آئے تھے
اب جائیں گے اوروں کو رُلا جائیں گے

اِس جہل کا ہے ذوؔق! ٹھکانہ کچھ بھی
ہم پڑھ کے ہوئے علم، نہ دانا کچھ بھی
ہم جانتے تھے، علم سے کچھ جانیں گے
جانا تو یہ جانا کہ نہ جانا کچھ بھی

کیا فائدہ فکرِ بیش و کم سے ہوگا
ہم کیا ہیں جو کوئی کام ہم سے ہوگا
جو کچھ کہ ہُوا، ہُوا کرم سے تیرے
جو کچھ ہوگا، تیرے کرم سے ہوگا

SHEIKH MOHAMMED IBRAHIM ZAUQ
(1789-1854)

We are here, O Zauq, to suffer the stings of woe;
Why we come, why we go, none doth really know;
Crying did we enter upon this worldly stage,
We'll leave others crying now as we go.

Duniya ke alam, Zauq, utha jaaenge,
Hum kya kahen kya aae the kya jaaenge,
Jab aae the hum rote hue aae the,
Ab jaaenge auron ko rula jaaenge.

This ignorance, O Zauq, all limits defies,
Despite all our learning, we remain unwise;
We were told learning would enlighten our hearts,
"We know naught" is all we know at the end of life.

Is jahal ka hai Zauq, thikana kuchh bhi,
Hum parh ke hue ilm, na danaa kuchh bhi;
Hum jaante the ilm se kuchh jaanenge,
Jaanaa to yeh jaana ke na jaanaa kuchh bhi.

Why should we worry in vain about loss or gain?
"We did this, we did that," who are we to claim?
Nothing was ever achieved without Thy grace divine,
Nor aught will ever be unless in Thy name.

Kya faaida fikr-e-besh-o-kam se hoga,
Hum kya hain jo koi kaam hum se hoga?
Jo kuchh ke hua, hua karam se tere,
Jo kuchh hoga, tere karam se hoga.

ذوق

دُنیا سے ذوق رشتۂ اُلفت کو توڑ دے
جس سِہر کا ہے یہ بال اُسی سرے سے جوڑ دے
پر تُو نہ ذوق چھوڑے گا اِس پیرِ زال کو
یہ پیرِ زال گر تجھے چاہے تو چھوڑ دے

آنکھ اس پرُ جفا سے لڑتی ہے
جان ، کُشتی قضا سے لڑتی ہے
زال دُنیا نے صُلح کی کس دِن
یہ لڑا کا سَدا سے لڑتی ہے

نِکلے ہوئے کدے سے ابھی منہ چھپا کے تُم
دابے ہوئے بغل میں صراحی شراب کی
اے ذوق بس نہ آپ کو صُوفی جتائیے
معلوم ہے حقیقتِ ہُو، حق ، جنابِ کی

Zauq

Snap the thread of love, O Zauq, that binds you to this world,
On its native head let this hair uncurl,
You'll not, I know, leave this hag, O Zauq,
Though this hag will one day leave you in the lurch.

Duniya se Zauq rishta-e-ulfat ko tor de,
Jis sar ka hai yeh baal usi sar se jor de;
Par tu na Zauq chhorega is pir zaal ko,
Yeh pir zaal gar tujhe chaahe to chhor de.

My eyes have clashed with that despot,
In a deadly duel my life is caught,
This hag of a world knows no peace,
This war-monger has fought and fought.

Aankh us purjafa se larti hai,
Jaan, kushti qazaa se karti hai,
Zaal duniya ne sulah ki kis din,
Yeh laraakaa sada se larti hai.

You have come out of tavern, guiltily, like a thief,
With the flask of wine, tucked under your sleeve,
Stop it now, O Zauq, withdraw your pious claims,
Your high-pitched hallelujahs can no longer deceive.

Nikle ho maikade se abhi munh chhipa ke tum,
Daabe hue baghal mein suraahi sharaab ki,
Ai Zauq bus na aapko sufi jataaeye,
Maalum hai haqiqat-e-hoo haq janaab ki.

ذوقؔ

اہلِ جوہر کو وطن میں رہنے دیتا گر فلک
لعل کیوں اِس رنگ سے آتا بدخشاں چھوڑ کر
اِن دنوں گرچہ دکن میں ہے بڑی قدرِ سخن
کون جائے ذوقؔ پر دِلّی کی گلیاں چھوڑ کر

آنکھیں کہیں کہ ”دل نے مجھے کر دیا خراب“
دِل نے کہا کہ ”آنکھوں نے مجھ کو ڈبا دیا“
بگڑا کسی کا کچھ نہیں اِس کشمکش میں ذوقؔ
دونوں کی ضِد نے خاک میں مجھ کو مِلا دیا

Zauq

Could talent live at home and thrive,
Why should the Badakhshaan-ruby thus wander worldwide?
Albeit in Deccan, Zauq, the Muse commands respect,
Who would quit the lanes of Delhi, and suffer exile?

Ahl-e-jauhar ko watan mein rahne deta gar falak,
Laal kyon is rung se aataa Badakhshaan chhor kar,
In dinon garche Dakan mein hai bari qadr-e-sakhun,
Kaun jaae Zauq par Dilli ki galiyan chhor kar.

Eyes complain, "Heart hath undone us complete,"
Heart bemoans? "Eyes have drowned me too deep,"
Neither, Zauq, has lost a fig in this tug-of-war,
Caught betwixt the warring two, I alone my fate beweep.

Aankhen kahen ke "dil ne mujhe kar diya kharaab,"
Dil ne kaha ke "aankhon ne mujh ko dabaa diya,"
Bigraa kisi ka kuchh nahin is kashmakash mein, Zauq,
Donon ki zid ne khaak mein mujhko mila diya.

مرزا اسداللہ خاں غالب

گھر ہمارا جو نہ روتے بھی تو ویراں ہوتا
بحر، گر بحر نہ ہوتا تو بیاباں ہوتا
تنگیٔ دل کا گِلہ کیا؟ یہ وہ کافردِل ہے
کہ اگر تنگ نہ ہوتا، تو پریشاں ہوتا

مشکل ہے زبس کلام میرا اے دِل
سُن سُن کے اِسے سُخن ورانِ کامل
آساں کہنے کی کرتے ہیں فرمائش
"گویم مشکل وگرنہ گویم مشکل"

سامان خور و خواب کہاں سے لاؤں
آرام کے اسباب کہاں سے لاؤں
روزہ مرا ایمان ہے غالب لیکن
خس خانہ و برفاب کہاں سے لاؤں

MIRZA ASADULLAH KHAN GHALIB
(1797-1869)

My house would have been wrecked even if I had not
   wept,
Had the sea been not the sea, a desert therein would have
   crept,
Rue not its narrowness, this infidel heart,
Had it not been narrow, would have been perplexed.

Ghar hamaara jo na rote bhi tau weeraan hota,
Bahr gar bahr na hota, tau beaabaan hota,
Tangi-e-dil ka gila kya, yeh woh kaafir dil hai,
Ke agar tung na hota, tau pareshaan hota.

Too hard to grasp is my verse, O heart!
Hearing it, the connoisseurs of art
For a simpler style do ask.
"Difficult, if I write, difficult, if do not."

Mushkil hai zabas kalaam mera ai dil,
Sun sun ke ise sukhanwaraan-e-kaamil,
Aasaan kahne ki karte hain farmaish,
"Goim mushkil wa gar na goim mushkil."

How to procure the means to sleep and feed?
Amenities of life my grasp exceed;
The holy fast, Ghalib, is a tenet of my faith,
But where to get a khas-cooled house, and ice to beat the
   heat?

Saamaan-e-khur-o-khwab kahaan se laun,
Aaraam ke asbaab kahaan se laun,
Roza mera imaan hai Ghalib lekin
Khas khanaa-o-barfaab kahaan se laun?

غالب

حاصل سے ہاتھ دھو بیٹھ، اے آرزوِ خرامی!
دل، جوشِ گریہ میں ہے ڈوبی ہوئی آسامی
اُس شمع کی طرح سے، جسکو کوئی بجھا دے
میں بھی، جلے ہوؤں میں، ہوں داغِ ناتمامی

تغافل دوست ہوں، میرا دماغِ عجز عالی ہے
اگر پہلو تہی کیجے، تو جا میری بھی خالی ہے
رہا آباد عالَم، اہلِ ہمّت کے نہ ہونے سے
بھرے ہیں جس قدر جام و سُبو، میخانہ خالی ہے

ہے وصل و ہجر، عالم تمکین و ضبط میں
معشوق شوخ و عاشقِ دیوانہ چاہیئے
اُس لب سے مل ہی جائیگا بوسہ کبھی تو، ہاں
شوقِ فضول و جرأتِ رندانہ چاہیئے

Ghalib

Wash your hands off the debt, O vain desire!
This tear-engulfed heart has bankrupt gone entire,
Like a candle, by someone snuffed alive,
I am a scalded heart, tending faded fire.

Haasil se haath dho beth, ai aarzoo-e-khiraami,
Dil josh-e-giriya mein hai doobi hui aasaami,
Us shama ki tarah se jisko koi bujha de,
Main bhi jale huon mein hun dagh-e-naa tamaami.

I am indifference prone, my humble head is high,
If I am pushed aside, void too my place shall lie;
The world remains abustle, no doubt, but without the
    valiant hearts,
Despite the brimming cups and cans, taverns desolate
    lie.

Taghaaful dost hun, mera dimagh-e-ijz aali hai,
Agar pahlu tahi keje, to meri jaa bhi khaali hai;
Rahaa aabaad aalam, ahl-e-himmat ke na hone se,
Bhare hain jisqadar jaam-o-sabu, maikhana khaali hai.

Union or severance inhere in passion and control,
What you need is a reckless lover and a darling cute;
Those lips will one day condescend to kiss,
All you need is a passion wild, and a mad pursuit.

Hai wasal-o-hijar, aalam-e-tamkeen-o-zabat mein,
Maashuq shokh wa aashiq-e-deewanaa chaaheye,
Us lab se mil hi jaaigaa bosa kabhi to, haan,
Shauq-e-fazul wa jurrat-e-rindaana chaaheye.

مومن خاں مومن

نہ صبر و سُکوں کا گھر میں یارا مجھکو
نے کوچہِ یار میں گذارا مجھکو
سیماب کی طرح ایک دَم چین نہیں
بیتابیِ دِل نے آہ ، مارا مجھکو

میں کیا کہوں اپنے مُنہ سے کیسے تم ہو
تم آپ ہی جانتے ہو جیسے تم ہو
ہرجائی اور ناقدرِ عُدو کو نہ کہو
کہہ بیٹھے کوئی مُبادا ایسے تم ہو

مومن لازم ہے وضع مرغوب بنے
جو رنگ ہو آدمی خوش اُسلوب بنے
کیا خرقہ و عمامہ ہے اللہ اللہ
جب شکل بگڑ گئی تو تم خوب بنے

MOMIN KHAN MOMIN
(1800-1852)

I cannot find at home the peace of mind I seek,
Nor doth my love's street offer me retreat;
Mercury-like I remain ever ill-at-ease,
My restlessness, alas, has undone me complete.

Na sabar-o-sakun ka ghar mein yaaraa mujko,
Ne kucha-e-yaar mein guzaaraa mujko,
Seemaab ki tarah ek dam chain nahin,
Betaabi-e-dil ne, aah, maaraa mujko.

How can I say on my own that you are this sort,
You know it full well what you really art,
Don't call the rival flirtatious, ingrate,
Lest you are hoisted with your own petard.

Main kya kahun apne munh se kaise tum ho,
Tum aap hi jaante ho, jaise tum ho,
Harjaai aur naa qadar adu ko na kaho,
Kah bethe koi mubaadaa aise tum ho.

Momin, it's important one should look smart,
One should in every state wear a goodly garb,
What tunic, what turban, by God, you support!
O, how you dress and deck, when native charms depart!

Momin, laazim hai wazaa marghub bane,
Jo rung ho aadmi khush-aslub bane,
Kya khirqa-o-ammaama hai Allah, Allah,
Jab shakal bigar gai tau tum khub bane.

مومن

یہ حکمِ خدا کا کہ قطرہ مے کا نہ پیوں
اور مرضیٔ جاناں کہ پیمانہ نہ پیوں
تو بھی ہے عزیزِ خاطر، ساقی بھی
حیران ہوں کہ پھر بادہ پیوں یا نہ پیوں

اب ہم پہ جو ہر گھڑی وہ جھنجھلاتے ہیں
الطافِ قدیم آہ یاد آتے ہیں
تھا یا تو وہ لطف یا یہ نفرت، اللہ
لوگ ایسے بھی دُنیا میں بدل جاتے ہیں

پروانے کو کس لیے جلایا اے شمع
بے جُرم کو خاک میں مِلایا اے شمع
سر کٹنے سے بھی ذرا شرارت نہ گئی
تُو نے تو غضب ہی سر اُٹھایا اے شمع

Momin

God forbids me to drink even a little drop,
Saqi wants I should drain away the draught;
I respect my Saqi, I revere my God,
To drink or not to drink—how should I resolve?

Yeh hukam Khudaa ka ke qatra mai ka na peeun,
Aur marzi-e-jaanaana ke paimaana peeun,
Tu bhi hai aziz-e-khaatir, Saqi bhi,
Hairaan hun ke phir baada peeun yaa na peeun.

Now at every moment when at me he frowns,
I recall the favours which once my heart did crown,
What a love, my God! by what a hate replaced!
How surprising, the folks can thus swing around.

Ab hum pe jo har ghari woh jhunjalaate hain,
Altaaf-e-qadim, ah, yaad aate hain,
Thaa yaa to woh lutaf, yaa yeh nafrat, Allah,
Log aise bhi duniya mein badal jaate hain.

What for, O taper, did you burn the moth?
Why mingled him in dust without a single fault?
You didn't shed your mischief though your head was
  chopped,
Awful and headstrong, you care not a jot.

Parwaane ko kis liye jalaayaa, ai shama,
Be juram ko khaak mein milaaya, ai shama,
Sar katne se bhi zara shararat na gai,
Tu ne tau ghazab hi sar uthaaya, ai shama.

مومن

رو رو کے کہا اُس سے مُلاقات کی رات
رو رو کے کٹیں ہجر کی راتیں ہیہات!
اب ذکرِ شبِ وصل ہے احباب سے اور
رونا ہی زار زار یہ ہے کیا بات

مومن نہیں زُہدِ بے ریا سے اُمّید
کیا شیخ ہوئی کسی دُعا سے اُمّید
جب رحم مُحبّت میں صنم نے نہ کیا
کیا عشقِ حقیقی میں خُدا سے اُمّید

احسان کیا اگر ستایا تُو نے
قصّہ سے نباہ کے چھڑایا تُو نے
کرنے لگے پھر و ہی سمجھ کی باتیں
بارے ہمیں آدمی بنایا تُو نے

Momin

In tears I told my love on the union night:
"All through the nights of severance I wept and sighed,
Now when I recount to friends the tale of union sweet,
Again my eyes swell with tears, what a queer plight!

Ro ro ke kaha us se mulaaqaat ki raat,
Ro ro ke katin hijar ki raaten, hehaat!
Ab zikar-e-shab-e-wasal hai ahbaab se, aur
Rona hi zaar zaar yeh hai kya baat.

Momin, I have no hope from piety, true and deep,
What profit from prayer, O priest, can we ever reap?
When I got no mercy from my love on earth,
How can the love celestial bring me better meed?

Momin, nahin zuhad-e-be riya se umeed,
Kya sheikh hoti kisi duaa se umeed,
Jab raham muhabbat mein sanam ne na kiya,
Kya ishq-e-haqiqi mein Khuda se umeed!

I feel beholden that you plagued my heart,
You have liberated me from the plighted troth;
Once again I talk like a sensible being,
You have made a man of me, kudos to your art!

Ahsaan kiya agar sataaya tu ne,
Qissa se nibaah ke chhuraaya tu ne,
Karne lage phir wohi samajh ki baaten,
Baare hamen aadmi banaaya tu ne.

مومن

وصلَت میں کبھی مزا نہ پایا ہم نے
عشق اِک فریب تھا کہ کھایا ہم نے
اے کاش کہ جان دِل سے پہلے دیتے
جی کے یہ عبَث عذاب اُٹھایا ہم نے

بدنام کیا تیرا بُرا ہو اے دِل
ناکام کیا تیرا بُرا ہو اے دِل
مومن کو بُتوں سے کیا سروکار بھلا
کیا کام کیا تیرا بُرا ہو اے دِل

مومن شوقِ گناہ گاری کب تک
اے تیرہ دَروں سیاہ کاری کب تک
جان اپنے خدُا کو، باز آ بہرِ خُدا
اے دُشمنِ دیں بُتوں سے یاری کب تک

Momin

I derived no pleasure from my amorous meets,
Love was a deceiving elf, which my heart did cheat,
I wish I'd given my life ere I gave my heart,
I only lived to undergo unnecessary griefs.

Waslat mein kabhi maza na payaa hum ne,
Ishq ek fareb tha ke khaaya hum ne,
Ai kaash ke jaan dil se pahle dete,
Ji ke yeh abas azaab uthaaya hum ne.

You have brought me disgrace, be thou cursed, my heart!
I am rendered useless, be thou cursed, my heart!
What had Momin, tell me, with idols got to do?
What a mischief ye have wrought, be thou cursed, my heart!

Badnaam kiya tera bura ho ai dil,
Naakaam kiya tera bura ho ai dil,
Momin ko buton se kya sarokaar bhala,
Kya kaam kiya tera bura ho ai dil.

How long, Momin, will you be to sinful life a thrall?
How long will you, O darkness prone, heed the evil call?
For God's sake, renounce evil, remember your Lord,
How long will the fleshly beauties be your bosom pal?

Momin, shauq-e-gunahgaari kab tak,
Ai teera darun seaah kaari kab tak,
Jaan apne Khuda ko, baaz aa bahr-e-Khuda,
Ai dushman-e-din, buton se yaari kab tak?

مِرزا سَلامت علی دبیؔر

پروانے کو دُھن، شمع کو لَو تیری ہے
عالَم میں ہر اک کو تنگ و دَد تیری ہے
مصباح، نجوم و آفتاب و مہتاب
جس نُور کو دیکھتا ہُوں، ضَو تیری ہے

کیا فِکرِ دوا خاکِ شفا کے ہوتے
چاندی کی تلاش کیمیا کے ہوتے
خاموش خلافِ بندگی ہے یہ دبیؔر
بندوں سے کہوں حال، خُدا کے ہوتے

نادان کہوں دل کو کہ خِردمند کہوں
یا سلسلۂ وضع کا پابند کہوں
اک روز خُدا کو مُنہ دِکھانا ہے دبیؔر
بندوں کو میں کس مُنہ سے خُداوند کہوں

MIRZA SALAMAT ALI DABIR
(1803-1875)

The yearning moth and the burning lamp both aspire for
   Thee,
Everyone in the world is questing none but Thee;
The taper, the stars, the sun and moon—
All that glows on this orb, draws its fire from Thee.

Parwane ko dhun, shama ko lau, teri hai,
Aalam mein har ik ko tag-o-daw, teri hai,
Masbaah, najum-o-aaftaab-o-mahtaab,
Jis nur ko dekhta hun zau teri hai.

Why worry about regimen, when the sacred dust is here,
When alchemy is at hand, why seek thou silver, dear?
This quiet, contented Dabir adulation abhors,
Why approach the humans when God the great is near?

Kya fikar-e-dawaa khaak-e-shifaa ke hote,
Chaandi ki talaash keemeya ke hote,
Khamosh khilaaf-e-bandgi hai yeh Dabir,
Bandon se kahun haal Khuda ke hote!

What should I call my heart, wise or unwise?
Or a mere prisoner of the code of life?
I have to face my God, O Dabir, one day,
How can the humans by me be deified?

Naadaan kahun dil ko ke khiradmand kahun,
Yaa silsalaa-e-wazaa ka paaband kahun,
Ik roz Khuda ko munh dikhanaa hai Dabir,
Bandon ko kis munh se main Khudawand kahun!

دبیر

اِک دن پیوندِ خاک ہونا ہوگا
تنہا تنہا لحد میں سونا ہوگا
اس قبر کے پردے کا کھلا حال دبیر
جو اوڑھنا ہوگا، وہ بچھونا ہوگا

ہم چشم بہت کم آشنا ہوتے ہیں
کب مردمِ دیدہ ایک جا ہوتے ہیں
یہ مجمعِ احباب غنیمت ہے دبیر
اِک بات میں دونوں لب جُدا ہوتے ہیں

صد حیف کہ پہلے سے نہ ہشیار ہوئے
آرامِ لحد کے نہ طلب گار ہوئے
ہنگامِ اجل آنکھ کھلی غفلت سے
جب سونے کا وقت آیا تو بیدار ہوئے

Dabir

We will lie buried in the dust at last,
Each one in his grave will sleep apart,
The truth of the grave has dawned on me, Dabir,
The sheet spread beneath will also wrap us fast.

Ik din paiwand-e-khaak hona hoga,
Tanhaa tanhaa lahd mein sona hoga,
Is qabar ke parde ka khula haal Dabir,
Jo orhna hoga woh bichhona hoga.

Men of equal status seldom close their ranks,
Have pupils of the eye ever shaken hand?
Count it a blessing, Dabir, this gathering of friends,
Utter but one word, the lips severed stand.

Hum chashm bahut kum aashna hote hain,
Kab mardam-e-deeda ek jaa hote hain,
Yeh majmaa-e-ahbaab ghanimat hai, Dabir,
Ik baat mein donon lab judaa hote hain.

Alas, alas, we did not in time awake,
The peace of the grave never did we crave,
Now that death holds us captive, we ope our eyes,
When its time to sleep, we begin to wake.

Sud haif ke pahle se na hushiaar hue,
Aaraam-e-lahad ke na talabgaar hue,
Hangaam-e-ajal aankh khuli ghaflat se,
Jab sone ka waqt aaya to bedaar hue.

دبیر

یہ عیش و نشاط و کامرانی کب تک؟
گر یہ بھی سہی تو نوجوانی کب تک؟
گر یہ بھی سہی، قرارِ دولت ہے محال
گر یہ بھی سہی، تو زندگانی کب تک؟

زردار نہیں اور طالبِ زر بھی نہیں
میں بے سر و پا کسی کا ہمسر بھی نہیں
پھر خاک میں مجھ کو کیوں ملاتا ہے فلک
میں کون ہوں، خاک کے برابر بھی نہیں

پیشِ اُمرا طالبِ زر جھکتے ہیں
سجدے کی طرح مجرے کو سر جھکتے ہیں
سنجیدہ ہیں یہ لوگ ترازو کی طرح
ہے مال سوا جدھر اُدھر جھکتے ہیں

Dabir

How long will you chase power and pelf?
How long tell me, will last your wealth?
Then, how long will your youth endure?
And how long, say, is life itself?

Yeh aish-o-nishaat-o-kaamraani kab tak,
Gar yeh bhi sahi to naujawaani kab tak,
Gar yeh bhi sahi, qarar-e-daulat hai mahaal,
Gar yeh bhi sahi, to zindgaani kab tak.

I am not a man of riches, nor for wealth I lust,
A challenge holds to none, this humble man accurst,
Why doth the sky raze me to the ground?
I'm not worth as much as the trodden dust.

Zardaar nahin aur talib-e-zar bhi nahin,
Main be sar-o-paa kisi ka humsar bhi nahin,
Phir khaak mein mujkho kyon milaata hai falak,
Main kaun hun, khaak ke baraabar bhi nahin.

The gold-greedy folk before the rich do bow,
In obeisance they fall, their heads sunk so low,
Thoughtful are these people, like the sensitive scales,
Whichever side is heavier, thither bends their brow.

Pesh-e-umraa taalib-e-zar jhukte hain,
Sajde ki tarah mujre ko sar jhukte hain,
Sanjeeda hain yeh log taraazu ki tarah,
Hai maal siwa jidhar udhar jhukte hain.

دبیر

یارانِ گزشتہ کی خبر خاک نہیں
ایسے ہی گئے کہ اب اثر خاک نہیں
چُن چُن کے کیا خاک ہُنرمندوں کو
اے چرخ! تجھے قدرِ ہُنر خاک نہیں

دُنیا کا عُجب کارخانہ دیکھا
کس کس کا نہ یاں ہم نے زمانہ دیکھا
برسوں رہا جن کے سر پہ چترِ زرّیں
تُربت پہ نہ اُن کی شامیانہ دیکھا

کس خوابِ تغافل میں یہاں سوتا ہے
کیوں مُفت متاعِ زندگی کھوتا ہے
تو حق سے لگا کہ صبح پیری آئی
ہُشیار! چراغِ عُمر گُل ہوتا ہے

Dabir

Lost and gone for ever are o'r former mates,
They've utterly vanished without leaving a trace,
One by one is wasted the entire gifted race,
O, heavens, you cannot talent appreciate.

Yaaraan-e-guzashta ki khabar khaak nahin,
Aise hi gaye ke ab asar khaak nahin,
Chun chun ke kiya khaak hunarmandon ko,
Ai charkh! tujhe qadar-e-hunar khaak nahin.

The workshop of this world is a strange place,
We have known the fate of several potentates,
Those who for years wore a crown of gold,
Do not have a canopy even arching over their graves.

Duniya ka ajib kaarkhaana dekha,
Kis kis ka na yaan hum ne zamaana dekha,
Barson raha jin ke sar pe chatar-e-zarrin,
Turbat pe na un ki shaamiaana dekha.

Why dost thou lazily dream your life away?
Why dost thou waste this wealth of night and day?
Get in tune with God, old age begins,
Awake, the lamp of life is about to fade away.

Kis khwaab-e-taghaaful mein yahaan sota hai,
Kyon muft mitaa-e-zindagi khota hai,
Lau haq se laga ke subah-e-piri aai,
Hushiaar, chiragh-e-umr gul hota hai.

دبیر

کِس عہد میں تبدیل نہیں دَور ہُوا
گہے عدل، گہے ظُلم، گہے جَور ہُوا
اللہ وُہی ہے تُو نہ مُضطر ہو دبیرؔ
کیا غم جو زمین و فلک اَور ہُوا

پہنچا جو کمال کو، وطن سے نکلا
قطرہ جو گُہر بنا، عدن سے نکلا
تکمیلِ کمال کی غریبی ہے دلیل
پختہ جو ثمر ہوا، چمن سے نکلا

Dabir

When have the times ever stayed unchanged?
Justice, oppression, tyranny, variously have ranged,
Don't feel perturbed, Dabir, when Eternal God is there,
It matters not if earth and sky now stand estranged.

Kis ahd mein tabdil nahin daur hua,
Gah adal, gahe zulam, gahe jaur hua,
Allah wohi hai tau na muztir ho Dabir,
Kya ghum jo zameen-o-falak aur hua.

You are externed from home when excellence you hit,
The drop turned a pearl its Aden has to quit,
Perfection necessitates exile from home,
When the fruit is ripe 'tis poised for exit.

Pahunchaa jo kamaal ko watan se nikla,
Qatra jo guhar bana aden se nikla,
Takmil kamaal ki gharibi hai dalil,
Pukhta jo samar hua chaman se nikla.

میر ببر علی انیس

گوہر کو صدف میں آبرو دیتا ہے
بندے کو بغیرِ جستجو دیتا ہے
انسان کو رِزق، گل کو بُو، سنگ کو لعل
جو کچھ دیتا ہے جس کو تُو دیتا ہے

گلُشن میں پھروں کہ سیرِ صحرا دیکھوں
یا معدن و کوہ و دشت و دریا دیکھوں
ہر جا تری قدرت کے ہیں لاکھوں جلوے
حیران ہوں کہ دو آنکھوں سے کیا کیا دیکھوں

آدم کو عجب خُدا نے رُتبا بخشا
ادنیٰ کے لیے مقامِ اعلیٰ بخشا
عقل و ہنر و تمیز و جان و ایمان
اس ایک کفِ خاک کو کیا کیا بخشا

MIR BABAR ALI ANEES
(1804-1874)

You bestow the precious glow on the coral pearl,
You provide the needs of man without strife or stir,
To man his bread, to flower perfume, rubies to the rocks
Whatever blessings we descry, Thy grace confers.

Gauhar ko sidaf mein aabru deta hai,
Bande ko baghair justjoo deta hai,
Insaan ko rizq, gul ko boo, sung ko laal,
Jo kuchh deta hai jisko, tu deta hai.

Should I roam the gardens through, or in deserts stroll,
Forests, rivers, mountains, mines,—what should I explore?
Everywhere Thy beauty a myriad shapes presents,
I wonder how with just two eyes, I could see the whole.

Gulshan mein phirun ke sair-e-sahraa dekhun,
Yaa maadan-e-koh-o-dasht-o-darya dekhun,
Har jaa teri qudrat ke hain laakhon jalwe,
Hairaan hun ke do aankhon se kya kya dekhun.

With a unique status is man by God blest,
On a puny creature a great rank is thrust,
Talent, sense and sentience, wisdom kindling faith,
All this and much more for a handful of dust!

Aadam ko ajab Khuda ne rutbaa bakhshaa,
Adnaa ke lieye maqaam-e-aalaa bakhshaa,
Aqal-o-hunar-o-tameez-o-jaan-o-imaan,
Is ek kaf-e-khaak ko kya kya bakhshaa!

انیس

رُتبہ جسے دیتا ہے خُدا دیتا ہے
وُہ دِل میں فروتنی کو جا دیتا ہے
کرتے ہیں تہی مغز شِناآپ اپنی
جو ظرف کہ خالی ہے صدا دیتا ہے

کِس مُنہ سے کہوں لائقِ تحسین مَیں ہُوں
کیا لُطف جو گُل کہے رنگین مَیں ہُوں
ہوتی ہے حلاوتِ سُخن خود ظاہر
کہتی ہے کہیں شکر کہ شیریں مَیں ہُوں

کیا کیا دُنیا سے صاحبِ مال گئے
دولت نہ گئی ساتھ، نہ اطفال گئے
پہونچا کے لحد تلک پھر آتے سب لوگ
ہمراہ اگر گئے، تو اعمال گئے

Anees

God is the giver of rank and place,
He fills the heart with humble grace;
Self-praise is the creed of hollow minds,
Empty vessels always a mighty tumult raise.

Rutbaa jise deta hai Khuda deta hai,
Woh dil mein faro-tani ko jaa deta hai,
Karte hain tahi maghz sanaa aap apni,
Jo zaraf ke khaali hai sadaa deta hai.

It doesn't behove me to sing my own praise,
Does the rose ever extol its own hue or grace?
The beauty of speech proves itself without being proclaimed,
Does sugar ever say, "I am sweet in taste?"

Kis munh se kahun laaiq-e-tahseen main hun,
Kya lutf jo gul kahe rangeen main hun,
Hoti hai halaawat-e-sukhun khud zaahir,
Kahti hai kahin shakar ke sheereen main hun!

How many men of pelf and pride have sunk into their grave,
Neither wealth nor children company to them gave,
The kith and kin return home from the burial place,
If anything, our deeds alone attend us beyond the grave.

Kya kya duniya se saahab-e-maal gaye,
Daulat na gai saath na itfaal gaye,
Pauhncha ke lahad talak phir aae sab log,
Hamraah agar gaye to aamaal gaye.

انیِس

خاموشی میں یاں لذّتِ گویائی ہے
آنکھیں جو ہیں بند، عین بینائی ہے
نے دوست کا جھگڑا ہے نہ دشمن کا فساد
مَرقَد بھی عجب گوشۂ تنہائی ہے

افسوس زمانے کا عجب طَور ہوا
کیوں چرخِ کہن کہن آج نیا دَور ہوا
بس یاں سے کہیں اور چلو جلد انیس
اب یاں کی زمیں اور فلک اور ہوا

سینے میں یہ دَم شمعِ سحرگاہی ہے
جو ہے اس کارواں میں، وہ راہی ہے
پیچھے کبھی قافلہ سے رہتا نہ انیس
اے عمرِ دراز تیری کوتاہی ہے

Anees

Speech-like tastes the silence here,
Eyes are closed, vision is clear,
No quarrel with friend, no fight with foe,
What a peaceful nook is the grave, O dear!

Khaamoshi mein yaan lazzat-e-goiaai hai,
Ankhen jo hain band ain beenaai hai,
Na dost ka jhagra hai, na dushman ka fasaad,
Marqad bhi ajab gosha-e-tanhaai hai!

The world now affects, alas, ways quite strange,
Eternal heavens, why have the times suddenly changed,
Let us quickly quit this place, and look for pastures new,
The earth and air now project an unfamiliar mein.

Afsos zamaane ka ajab taur hua,
Kyon charkh-e-kuhan, aaj naya daur hua,
Bus yaan se kahin aur chalo jald, Anees,
Ab yaan ki zamin aur falak aur hua.

The breath within the breast is the flickering lamp of dawn,
Travellers are we all who form this caravan,
Anees would never have lagged behind his mates,
Because of you, O long life, he trails the marathon.

Seene mein yeh dam shama-e-sahr gaahi hai,
Jo hai is carvan mein woh raahi hai,
Peechhe kabhi qaafla se rahta na Anees,
Ai umr-e-daraaz teri kotaahi hai.

انیس

کیوں زر کی ہوس میں دربدر پھرتا ہے
جانا ہے تجھے کہاں ہے کدھر پھرتا ہے؟
اللہ رے پیری میں ہوس، دُنیا کی
تھک جاتے ہیں جب پاؤں تو سر پھرتا ہے

عزّت رہے یارو آشنا کے آگے
محجُوب نہ ہوں شاہ و گدا کے آگے
یہ پاؤں چلیں تو راہِ مَولا میں چلیں
جب ہاتھ یہ اُٹھیں تو خُدا کے آگے

دُنیا بھی عجب سرائے فانی دیکھی
ہر چیز یہاں کی آنی جانی دیکھی
جو آکے نہ جائے وہ بڑھاپا دیکھا
جو جاکے نہ آئے وہ جوانی دیکھی

Anees

Why this hectic race for the greed of gold?
Whither dost thou wander, whither is thy goal?
Oh, this lust for worldly things in this hoary age,
When feet get fatigued, wits lose their hold.

Kyon zar ki hawas mein dar badar phirta hai,
Jaana hai tujhe kahaan, kidhar phirta hai,
Allah re piri mein hawas duniya ki,
Thak jaate hain jab paaon tau sar phirta hai.

May God preserve my honour in the face of friends,
Let me not bend before the poor or affluent,
I should tread the path shown by Gracious God,
To Him alone I should these my hands extend!

Izzat rahe yaar-o-aashna ke aage,
Mahjub na hon shah-o-gada ke aage,
Yeh paaon chalen to raah-e-maula mein chalen,
Jab haath yeh uthen to Khuda ke aage.

Strange is this inn, a mere shifting show,
Where all things simply come and go,
Youth once gone never doth return,
But old age arrives never to go.

Duniya bhi ajab sarai faani dekhi,
Har cheez yahaan ki aani jaani dekhi,
Jo aake na jaae woh burhaapa dekha,
Jo jaa ke na aae woh jawaani dekhi.

عبدالعلیم آسی غازی پوری

ہر چند کہ موت کا طلب گار ہُوں میں
رنج و الم و غم سے گراں بار ہُوں میں
پر زندگی اپنی کہہ چکا ہُوں تجھ کو
کس مُنہ سے کہوں زیست سے بیزار ہُوں میں

اِک عمر رہِ طلب میں چکّر کھایا
آخر دِل میں سُراغ اِس کا پایا
دِل میں دیکھا تو آئینے کی صُورت
جُز اپنے کوئی نظر نہ مُجھ کو آیا

کرتا رہوں میں تو یُوں فغان و زاری
اُس بُت کے نہ دل میں رحم ہو یا باری
پتھّر سہی دِل مگر پسیجے نہیں کیوں
پتھر سے تو ہوتے ہیں دریا جاری

ABDUL ALEEM AASI GHAZIPURI
(1834-1917)

Though I surely long for death,
Griefs and troubles me do fret,
Having said, "You are my life,"
How can I say, "My life I dread?"

Har chand ke maut ka talabgaar hun main,
Ranj-o-alam-o-ghum se garaanbaar hun main,
Par zindagi apni kah chuka hoon tujh ko,
Kis munh se kahun, zeest se bezaar hun main!

All my life I was obsessed with His quest,
At last in my heart His prints I found imprest,
When I gazed at my heart, serving as a mirror,
None but me could I see lurking in this nest.

Ik umr rah-e-talab mein chakkar khaya,
Aakhir dil mein suraagh uska paaya,
Dil mein dekha to aaeene ki surat,
Juz apne koi nazar na mujhko aaya.

I'll continue to weep and wail,
Let it not move his heart or tears entail,
Even if his heart be stone, why shouldn't it melt,
From the heart of rocks itself, the rivers often hail.

Karta rahun main tau yun fughaan-o-zaari,
Us but ke na dil mein raham ho yaa baari,
Paththar sahi dil magar paseeje nahin kyon,
Paththar se tau hote hain darya jaari.

آسی غازی پوری

اِک روز کہا میَں نے کہ تُو دِلبرَ ہَے
جانِ عاشق ، لَبِ شَکر پَرور ہَے
کِس ناز سے بولے مُنہ کو مُنہ پر رکھ کر
اب یہ کہئے کہ جان ہونٹوں پر ہے

کیوں نقطۂ موہوم بنایا ہمکو
کیوں دائرۂ فنا میں لایا ہمکو
وُہ سہو نویس تھا ، نہ ہم حرفِ غلط
کیوں صفحۂ ہستی سے مِٹایا ہمکو

Aasi

"You are," I told him, "the object of my heart,"
"You are the lover's life, your lips honey discharge,"
Placing his mouth on my mouth, how cutely he quipped,
"Lo my life is on my lips," you should now remark.

Ik roz kaha main ne ke tu dilbar hai,
Jaan-e-aashiq, lab-e-shakar-parwar hai,
Kis naaz se bole, munh ko munh par rakh kar,
Ab yeh kaheye ke jaan honton par hai.

Why was I made a vanishing dot?
Why assigned a mortal lot?
He was not a faulty hand, nor I a redundant mark,
Why was I rubbed off from life like a dirty spot?

Kyon nukta-e-mauhoom banaaya hum ko,
Kyon daaira-e-fana mein laya hum ko,
Woh sahw nawis tha, na hum haraf-e-ghalat,
Kyon safa-e-hasti se mitaaya hum ko?

خواجہ الطاف حسین حالی

پَستی کا کوئی حد سے گذرنا دیکھے
اِسلام کا گر کم نہ اُبھرنا دیکھے
مانے نہ کبھی کہ مَد ہے جَزَر کے بعد
دریا کا ہمارے جو اُترنا دیکھے

موسیٰ نے یہ کی عرض کہ اے بارِ خدا
مقبولؔ تِرا کون ہے بندوں میں سِوا
اِرشاد ہوا، بندہ ہمارا وہ ہے
جو لے سکے، اور نہ لے بدی کا بدلہ

اِک مُنعِم مصرف نے یہ عابد سے کہا
کر میرے لیے حق سے فراغت کی دُعا
عابد نے کہا ہاتھ اُٹھا کر سُوئے چرخ
محتاج کر اُس کو جلد بارِ خدا

KHWAJA ALTAF HUSSAIN HALI
(1837-1914)

Behold the degradation sinking far too deep,
Oh, the fall of Muslims, gone beyond retrieve;
You'll deny that each ebb is followed by the flow,
If our river, run stark dry, you once perceive.

Pasti ka koi had se guzarna dekhe,
Islaam ka gir kar na ubharna dekhe;
Maane na kabhi ke mad hai jazar ke baad,
Darya ka hamaare jo utarna dekhe.

Moses once asked God with humble concern,
Who among the humans, Lord, your utmost love may
    earn?
The Lord replied: "He alone is my faithful son,
"Who can, but doth not, an evil turn return."

Musa ne yeh ki arz ke ai baar-e-Khuda,
Maqbul tera kaun hai bandon mein siwa,
Irshaad hua banda hamaara woh hai,
Jo le sake, aur na le badi ka badla.

Thus spoke a busy rich to a saint one day:
For the grant of leisure, for me kindly pray;
Raising his hands to the sky the saint begged aloud:
"Make him destitute, O God, without least delay."

Ik munim-e-musraf ne yeh aabid se kaha,
Kar mere lieye haq se faraaghat ki duaa;
Aabid ne kaha haath utha kar su-e-charakh:
Muhtaaj kar isko jald baar-e-Khuda.

حاتی

یاں رہنے کی مہلت کوئی کب پاتا ہے؟
آتا ہے اگر آج تو کَل جاتا ہے
جو کرنے ہیں کام اُن کو جلدی بُھگتاؤ
طلبی کا پیام وُہ چلا آتا ہے

دولت نے کہا، مجھ سے ہے، عزّتِ جہاں
فرمایا ہُنر نے، مَیں ہُوں عزّت کا نِشاں
عزّت بولی، غلط ہے دونوں کا بیاں
مَیں بھید ہُوں حق کا جو ہے نیکی میں نہاں

کیا فرق؟ سماعت نہ ہو جب کانوں میں
دانائی کی باتوں میں اور افسانوں میں
غُربت میں ہے اجنبی مسافر جس طرح
دانا کا یہی حال ہے نادانوں میں

Hali

Who is permitted in the world for long to stay?
You must return tomorrow, if you come today.
Dispose them of, without delay, the tasks you undertake,
Lo, the herald with your summons cometh fast this way.

Yaan rahne ki muhlat koi kab paataa hai,
Aataa hai agar aaj to kal jaataa hai,
Jo karne hain kaam unko jaldi bhugtaao,
Talbi ka payaam woh chala aataa hai.

Wealth declared: "I'm the cause of honour everywhere."
Talent said, "None but I the badge of honour wear,"
Honour remarked: "Both of you are quite off the mark,
"I'm the God's secret, which goodness alone doth share."

Daulat ne kaha, mujhse hai, izzat hai jahaan,
Farmaaya hunar ne, main hun izzat ka nishaan,
Izzat boli, ghalat hai donon ka bayaan,
Main bhed hun haq ka jo hai neki mein nihaan.

If your ears cannot hear, what difference it makes,
Whether someone wisely talks, or fairy tales narrates,
As a lone traveller lost in alien lands,
The wise amidst the foolish, lives in such a state.

Kya farq samaat na ho jab kaanon mein,
Daanaai ki baaton mein aur afsaanon mein,
Ghurbat mein hai ajnabi musaafir jis tarah,
Daanaa ka yehi haal hai naadaanon mein.

حاآتی

دھونے کی ہے اے رفا گرم جا باقی
کپڑے پہ ہے جب تلک کہ دھبّا باقی
دھو شوق سے دھبّے کو پہ اِتنا نہ رگڑ
دھبّا رہے کپڑے پہ نہ کپڑا باقی

ممکن نہیں یہ کہ ہو بشر عیب سے دُور
ہر عیب سے بچئے تا بمقدُور ضرُور
عیب اپنے گھٹاؤ، پُر خبردار رہو
گھٹنے سے کہیں اُنکے نہ بڑھ جائے غرُور

ہے جہل میں سب عالم و جاہل ہمسر
آتا نہیں فرق اِسکے سوا اُن میں نظر
عالم کو ہے عِلم اپنی نادانی کا
جاہل کو نہیں جہل کی کچھ اپنے خبر

Hali

O, reformer, there is the need to scrub on your part,
So long as the cloth retains the dirty spot;
Wash the stain with pleasure, but scrub not so hard,
That both the stain and texture might come to naught.

Dhone ki hai ai reformer jaa baaqi,
Kapre pe hai jab talak ke dhabba baaqi,
Dho shauq se dhabbe ko pe itna na ragar,
Dhabba rahe kapre pe na kapra baaqi.

It's beyond the reach of man to purge himself of faults,
Yet you should try your best to shun the evil path,
Refine your faults by any means, nonetheless beware!
Lest you develop the sin of pride, and overshoot the mark.

Mumkin nahin yeh ke ho bashar aib se dur,
Har aib se bacheye taa bamaqdur zarur,
Aib apne ghataao, par khabar daar raho,
Ghatne se kahin unke na barh jaae gharur.

The learned and the ignorant are equal in some sense,
In the amount of ignorance there's small difference;
The learned knows full well what he does not know,
The ignorant is ignorant of his ignorance.

Hai jehal mein sab aalim-o-jaahil humsar,
Aata nahin farq iske siwa un mein nazar,
Aalim ko hai ilam apni naadaani ka,
Jaahil ko nahin jehal ki kuchh apne khabar.

ماں

جب مایوسی دلوں پہ چھا جاتی ہے
دُشمن سے بھی نام ِ ترا جپواتی ہے
ممکن ہے کہ شکم میں بھُول جائیں اطفال
لیکن اُنھیں دُکھ میں ماں ہی یاد آتی ہے

ہے عشق طبیب دل کے بیماروں کا
یا گھر ہے وہ خود ہزار آزاروں کا
ہم کچھ نہیں جانتے ، پہ اِتنی ہے خبر
اِک مشغلہ دلچسپ ہے بیکاروں کا

زاہد کہتا تھا جان ہے دین پہ قربان
پر آیا جب امتحان کی زد پر ایمان
کی عرض کسی نے ، کہئے اب کیا ہے صلاح
فرمایا کہ بھائی جان ، جی ہے تو جہان

Hali

When despair our hearts doth maul,
Atheists too Thy name recall;
Children might forget their mother in prosperous days;
They cannot but think of her when hard times appal.

Jab maayusi dilon pe chhaa jaati hai,
Dushman se bhi naam tera japwaati hai;
Mumkin hai ke sukh mein bhul jaaen itfaal,
Lekin unhein dukh mein maan hi yaad aati hai.

Is love the physician of ailing hearts,
Or a breeding place of ills unthought?
We do not know for certain, this much we know,
Love is a fine pursuit for the idle sort.

Hai ishq tabib dil ke beemaaron ka,
Yaa ghar hai woh khud hazaar aazaaron ka,
Hum kuchh nahin jaante, pe itni hai khabar,
Ik mashghala dilchasp hai bekaaron ka.

"My life is but pledged to faith," so the priest would say,
When the time arrived his claim to weigh,
Someone quietly asked, "What, sir, do you say?"
The priest replied, "Brother dear! life is the world's stay."

Zaahid kahta thaa jaan hai din pe qurbaan,
Par aaya jab imtahaan ki zad par imaan,
Ki arz kisi ne, kaheye ab kya hai salaah,
Farmaaya ke bhai jaan, ji hai to jahaan.

حالی

عشرت کا ثمر تلخ سدا ہوتا ہے
ہر قہقہہ پیغامِ بُکا ہوتا ہے
جس قوم کو عیش دوست پاتا ہوں
کہتا ہوں کہ اب دیکھئے کیا ہوتا ہے

تیمور نے اِک مورچہ زیرِ دیوار
دیکھا کہ چڑھا دانہ کو لے کر سَو بار
آخر سرِ بام لے کے پہنچا تو کہا
"مشکل نہیں کوئی پیشِ ہمّت دُشوار"

دُنیائے دُنی کو نقشِ فانی سمجھو
رُوداد جہاں کو اِک کہانی سمجھو
پر جب کرو آغاز کوئی کام بڑا
ہر سانس کو عمرِ جاودانی سمجھو

Hali

Luxury bitter fruit doth yield,
Laughter lamentation breeds,
On seeing a nation luxury prone,
I wonder where it all may lead.

Ishrat ka samar talakh sada hota hai,
Har qahqaha paighaam-e-bukaa hota hai,
Jis qaum ko aish dost paataa hun,
Kahta hun ke ab dekheye kya hota hai.

Tamur saw an ant scramble up a wall,
Many a time it tried to lift a grain and crawl,
When at last it reached the top, Tamur thus remarked:
"A strong will shall find no wall too tall."

Tamur ne ik morcha zer-e-diwaar,
Dekha ke charhaa daana ko le ke sau baar,
Aakhir sar-e-baam le ke pahuncha to kaha,
"Mushkil nahin koi pesh-e-himaat dushwaar."

Treat this world as transient, frail,
The voyage of life, a dream, a tale;
But when a noble work you start,
Trust that breath shall never fail.

Duniya-e-duni ko naqash-e-faani samjho,
Roodaad-e-jahaan ko ik kahaani samjho,
Par jab karo aaghaaz koi kaam bara,
Har saans ko umr-e-jaavdaani samjho.

اکبر حسین اکبر الہ آبادی

بے پردہ کل جو آئیں نظر چند بیبیاں
اکبر زمین میں غیرتِ قومی سے گڑ گیا
پوچھا جو اُن سے آپ کا پردہ وُہ کیا ہوا
کہنے لگیں کہ عقل پہ مردوں کی پڑ گیا

میرے منصوبے ترقی کے ہوُئے سب پایمال
بیج مغرب نے جو بویا وُہ اُگا اور پھل گیا
بوُٹ ڈاسن نے بنایا میں نے اِک مضمون لکھا
ملک میں مضمون نہ پھیلا اور جوُتا چل گیا

جو کہا میَں نے کہ پیار آتا ہے مجھُ کو تم پُر
ہنس کے کہنے لگے واور آپ کو آتا کیا ہے،
عام الزام ہے اکبر پہ کہ پیتا کیوں ہے
اس کی پُرسش نہیں ہوتی کہ کھاتا کیا ہے

AKBAR HUSSAIN KHAN AKBAR ALLAHABADI (1846-1921)

When Akbar saw some dames going about unveiled,
Hurt was his national pride, humbled was his head;
"What happened to your veil?" he asked, pat replied the dames:
"On the wits of gentlemen, it now lies spread."

Be purdah kal jo aain nazar chand bibiaan,
Akbar zameen mein ghairat-e-qaumi se gar gaya,
Puchha jo un se aap ka purdah woh kya hua,
Kahne lagin ke aqal pe mardon ki par gaya.

All my plans of progress have withered in the root,
The seed sown by the West has yielded fruit;
Dasan manufactured shoes, I wrote reviews;
Reviews remained unread, shoes were freely used.

Mere mansube taraqqi ke hue sab paaemaal,
Beej maghrib ne jo boya woh uga aur phal gaya,
Boot Dasan ne banaaya, main ne ik mazmun likha,
Mulak mein mazmun na phailaa, aur jootaa chal gaya.

When I said I've fallen deep in love with you,
Smilingly he quipped: "What else can you?"
Every one complains, why does Akbar drink?
The question, what he eats, none doth pursue.

Jo kaha main ne ke payaar aataa hai mujh ko tum par,
Hans ke kahne lage: "aur aap ko aataa kya hai!"
Aam ilzaam hai Akbar pe ke peetaa hai kyon,?
Is ki pursish nahin hoti ke khaataa kya hai.

اکبر

پرُانی روشنی میں اور نئی میں فرق اِتنا ہے
اُسے کشتی نہیں ملتی اِسے ساحل نہیں ملتا
کتابِ دل مجھے کافی ہے اکبر درسِ حکمت کو
میں اسپنسر سے مُستغنی ہُوں مجھ سے مل نہیں ملتا

خواہانِ نوکری نہ رہیں طالبانِ علم
قائم ہوئی ہے رائے یہ اہلِ شعور کی
کالج میں دُھوم مچ رہی ہے پاس پاس کی
عہدوں سے آ رہی ہے صدا دُور دُور کی

چھوڑ لٹریچر کو اپنی ہسٹری کو بھُول جا
شیخ و مسجد سے تعلق ترک کر، اسکول جا
چار دن کی زندگی ہے، کوفت سے کیا فائدہ
کھا ڈبل روٹی، کلرکی کر، خوشی سے پھُول جا

Akbar

This is what differentiates cultures new and old,
One has no shore in sight, the other lacks the oar;
The book of heart, Akbar, contains the finest lore,
I take my cue from Spenser, Mill, I ignore.

Puraani raushani mein aur nayee mein farq itna hai,
Use kashti nahin milti, ise saahil nahin milta;
Kitaab-e-dil mujhe kaafi hai, Akbar, dars-e-hikmat ko,
Main Spenser se mustaghni hun, mujh se Mill nahin milta.

The students are well-advised not to look for posts,
Such is the considered view of the learned folks,
The college is resounding with the re-iterated: "Passed!"
The offices are putting up, "No Vacancy" boards.

Khwahaan-e-naukri na rahen taalbaan-e-ilm,
Qaayam hui hai rai yeh ahl-e-shaoor ki,
College mein dhoom much rahi hai paas, paas ki,
Uhdon se aa rahi hai sada dur, dur ki.

Forget about literature, history over-rule,
Break with the priest and mosque, go, attend the school,
Short is the span of life, why sweat and strain?
Feed on bread, be a clerk, rejoice to the full.

Chhor literature ko apni, history ko bhool ja,
Sheikh-o-masjid se taalluq tark kar, school ja,
Chaar din ki zindagi hai, koft se kya faayda,
Kha double roti, clerky kar, khushi se phul ja.

اکبر

شیخ اپنی رگ کو کیا کریں ریشے کو کیا کریں
مذہب کے جھگڑے چھوڑیں تو پیشے کو کیا کریں
فرہاد سے کہا مناسب ہے تجھ کو صبر
کہنے لگا بتائیے تیشے کو کیا کریں

ہم اُردو کو عربی کیوں نہ کریں ہندی کو وہ بھاشا کیوں نہ کریں
جھگڑے کے لیے اخباروں میں مضمون تراشا کیوں نہ کریں
آپس میں عداوت کچھ بھی نہیں لیکن اک اکھاڑا قائم ہے
جب اِس سے فلک کا دل بہلے ہم لوگ تماشا کیوں نہ کریں

دولت بھی ہے، فلسفہ بھی ہے، جاہ بھی ہے
لطفِ حُسنِ بُتانِ دل خواہ بھی ہے
سب سے قطعِ نظر ہے مشکل، لیکن
اِتنا سمجھے رہو کہ اللہ بھی ہے

Akbar

What should the priest about his grain and fibre do?
If he renounces religious wrangling, his trade perishes too,
When Farhad was advised to act with restraint,
"Tell me, what," he asked, "with this pick-axe should I do?"

Sheikh apni rug ko kya karen, reshe ko kya karen,
Mazhab ke jhagre chhoren to peshe ko kya karen;
Farhaad se kaha munaasib hai tujh ko sabr,
Kahne laga bataaeye teeshe ko kya karen.

Why shouldn't we leaven Urdu with Arabic, why shouldn't they Hindi Sanskritize?
Why shouldn't we write for the press, and communal strife incite?
We have opened the battle front though cause for quarrel is none,
When people love watching the show, we cannot but oblige.

Hum Urdu ko Arbi kyon na karen, Hindi ko woh bhaasha kyon na karen,
Jhagre ke lieye akhbaaron mein mazmun taraasha kyon na karen;
Aapas mein adaawat kuchh bhi nahin, lekin ik akhaara qaayam hai,
Jab is se falak ka dil bahle, hum log tamaasha kyon na karen.

Wealth, rank, philosophy—you have all the three,
Beauties dearly loved and sought also run to thee;
You cannot dismiss them all, let's all agree,
Remember withal, there's a God, who created thee and me.

Daulat bhi hai, falsafa bhi hai, jaah bhi hai,
Lutaf-e-husan-e-butaan-e-dil-khwah bhi hai,
Sub se qata nazar hai mushkil, lekin,
Itna sumjhe raho ke Allah bhi hai.

علی مُحمّد شاد عظیم آبادی

کیا مُفت کا زاہدوں نے الزام لیا
تسبیح کے دانوں سے عبث کام لیا
یہ نام تو وُہ ہے جسے بے گنتی لیں
کیا لُطف جو گِن گِن کے ترا نام لیا

کیوں کم نہ رہے غمِ نہانی تیرا
دُنیا میں بتا کون ہے ثانی تیرا
ہم لے کے عصا دُور تلک ڈھونڈ آئے
کوسوں نہیں نام اَے جوانی تیرا

مُجھ سا کوئی دُنیا میں بدانجام نہیں
جُز شغلِ گُناہ اور کوئی کام نہیں
مَیں حرفِ غلط ہُوں صفحۂ عالم پر
گر کوئی مٹائے تو کوئی الزام نہیں

SAYED ALI MOHAMMED SHAD AZIMABADI (1846-1927)

Why should the priests have thus incurred the blame?
Why should they count the beads to praise His gracious name?
We should repeat His name without keeping count,
Why turn this sacred task into a counting game?

Kya muft ka zaahidon ne ilzaam liya,
Tasbeeh ke daanon se abas kaam liya,
Yeh naam to woh hai jise be ginti lein,
Kya lutaf jo gin gin ke tera naam liya.

Your grief within me doth embedded lie,
Where can I find, O Youth, your match under the sky?
Far and wide have I ranged with a staff in hand,
For miles I couldn't your footprints descry.

Kyon kar na rahe ghum-e-nihaani tera,
Duniya mein bata kaun hai saani tera,
Hum le ke asaa dur talak dhoond aae,
Koson nahin naam, ai jawaani tera.

The world cannot show a man as bad as I,
Save committing sins I did nothing in life,
I am a word redundant on the earth's page,
No harm if someone rubs me off outright.

Mujh saa koi duniya mein bud anjaam nahin,
Juz shaghul-e-gunaah aur koi kaam nahin,
Main haraf-e-ghalat hun safah-e-aalam par,
Gar koi mitaae to koi ilzaam nahin.

شادؔ عظیم آبادی

دُنیا ہے عجب اِک تماشا خانہ
سمجھا ہے اِسے جِس نے وُہ ہے فرزانہ
ظاہر میں ہو ارتباط و اُلفت سب سے
باطن میں بہ ہر طور رہے بیگانہ

جب تک ہے یہ جسم ایک گرفتاری ہے
جب رُوح جُدا ہوئی سبک باری ہے
جینا کہتے ہیں جسکو ہے خوابِ گراں
مرنا کیا شے ہے؟ عین بیداری ہے

اِس بزم سے دم بھر بھی نہ رُوپوش ہُوئے
ہم صحبتِ یارانِ قدح نوشش ہُوئے
ہلتی رہی شمع کی طرح مُنہ میں زبان
آخر ہم جل بُجھے تو خاموش ہُوئے

Shad Azimabadi

The world is a playhouse, deceptive and strange,
He who realizes this, among the wise doth range,
Though we meet and greet, and live in apparent peace,
In the heart of hearts we feel estranged.

Duniya hai ajab ik tamaasha khaana,
Samjha hai ise jis ne woh hai furzaana,
Zaahir mein ho irtabaat-o-ulfat sab se,
Baatan mein ba-har taur rahe begaana.

So long as the body lasts, fettered lie our feet,
When the soul quits the body, 'tis great relief,
Life is nothing but a dream profound,
Death may be called: awakening complete.

Jab tak hai yeh jisam, ek griftaari hai,
Jab rooh juda hui subak baari hai,
Jeena kahte hain jisko, hai khwaab-e-giraan,
Murna kya shai hai? ain bedaari hai.

We did not leave the sensuous throng even for a while,
Drowned in drunken revels we spent our life,
Our tongue kept flapping like the candle flame,
When completely burnt out, we became tongue-tied.

Is bazm se dum bhur bhi na roo-posh hue,
Hum suhbat-e-yaaraan-e-qadah nosh hue,
Hilti rahi shama ki tarah munh mein zabaan,
Aakhir hum jal bujhe to khaamosh hue.

شادؔ عظیم آبادی

ساقی کے کرم سے فیض یہ جاری ہے
یا پیرِ خرابات کی غم خواری ہے
صف توڑ کے بٹ رہی ہے رِندوں کو
معلوم نہیں کہ میری کب باری ہے

بدلے نہ صداقت کا نشاں ایک رہے
ہر حال میں پنہاں وعیاں ایک رہے
اِنسان ہے وُہی جو اِس دو رنگی سے بچے
لازم ہے کہ دل اور زباں ایک رہے

کیوں زیست سے نفرت ہمیں ہر دم نہ رہے
دِل جن سے قوی تھا اب وُہ ہمدم نہ رہے
ہنستے بھی ہیں شادؔ، بول بھی لیتے ہیں
ہم ہیں تو وُہی شادؔ، پہ وُہ ہم نہ رہے

Shad Azimabadi

This generous feast is laid out by the Saqi's grace,
Or, the tavern keeper's favours here lie displayed,
The revellers are being served out of turn today,
Who knows when my turn arrives, so the cup comes my way.

Saqi ke karam se faiz yeh jaari hai,
Yaa peer-e-kharaabaat ki ghum-khwaari hai,
Saf tor ke bat rahi hai rindon ko,
Maalum nahin ke meri kab baari hai.

It's the mark of truth to remain unchanged,
Seeing and being ever the same,
Duplicity doesn't behove a man,
The tongue should say what the heart proclaims.

Badle na sadaaqat ka nishaan ek rahe,
Har haal mein pinhaan-o-ayaan ek rahe,
Insaan hai wohi jo is dorangi se bache,
Laazim hai ke dil aur zabaan ek rahe.

Why shouldn't I this earthly life decry?
The friends who warmed my heart, I no longer espy,
Though, Shad, I speak as well as laugh,
I'm the self-same "I", yet different from that "I".

Kyon zeest se nafrat hamen har dum na rahe,
Dil jin se qawi tha ab woh humdum na rahe,
Hanste bhi hain, Shad, bole bhi lete hain,
Hum hain to wohi Shad, pe woh hum na rahe.

شاد عظیم آبادی

وہ سوچ لے ہر طرح سے جو بزم میں آئے
ایسا نہ ہو این و آں میں یُوں ہی رہ جائے
ساقی نے تو بھر کے رکھ دیا، اُس کو کیا
ساغر ہے اُسی مست کا جو ہاتھ بڑھائے

آنکھیں نہ کھُلیں، وہ کم نگاہی نہ گئی
وہ کینہ کشی، وہ کینہ خواہی نہ گئی
پیری نے تو بالوں کو کیا آ کے سفید
افسوس مگر دِل کی سیاہی نہ گئی

Shad Azimabadi

He who joins the feast, let him beware!
Lest he vacillates and misses the fare,
The Saqi fills the cup; he cares no more,
The cup is for him, who can claim his share.

Woh soch le har tarah se jo bazm mein aae,
Aisaa na ho een-o-aan mein yun hi rah jaae,
Saqi ne to bhar ke rakh diya, usko kya?
Saaghar hai usi must ka jo haath barhaae.

Myopic is our vision, sealed are our eyes,
We are still steeped in jealousy and pride,
Old age, albeit, has whitened our hair,
Black remains our heart, old age despite.

Aankhen na khulin, woh kum nigaahi na gai,
Woh keena kashi, woh keena khwaahi na gai,
Peeri ne tau baalon ko kiya aake safed,
Afsos magar dil ki sayaahi na gai.

سورج نارائن مہر

جس طرح سے مہر چھوڑ کر رختِ کہن
کر لیتے ہیں ہم جامۂ نَو زیبِ بدن
کرتی ہے حلول اور جسموں میں رُوح
ہو جاتا ہے کہنہ جب کہ یہ جامۂ تن

اپنا دیکھا ہے اور پرایا ہم نے
سَو بار ہے سب کو آزمایا ہم نے
اے مہر بنی کا ہے زمانہ ساتھی
بگڑی کا کوئی یار نہ پایا ہم نے

ہر شے میں جمالِ دلرُبا کو دیکھا
ہر چیز میں شانِ کبریا کو دیکھا
مخلوق میں خالق نظر آیا جس کو
اُس دیکھنے والے نے خدا کو دیکھا

SURAJ NARAIN MEHAR
(1859-1931)

As we, discarding worn out clothes,
Dress ourselves in newest robes,
The soul, abandoning bodies old,
Enshrines herself in fresh abodes.

Jistareh se, Mehar, chhor kar rakht-e-kuhan,
Kar lete hain hum jaama-e-nau zeb-e-badan,
Karti hai halul aur jismon mein rooh,
Ho jaata hai kuhna jab yeh jaama-e-tan.

We have seen strangers, we have known friends,
Have tried them both times without end,
In golden days we are wooed by all,
In days adverse none is our friend.

Apna dekha hai aur paraaya hum ne,
Sau baar hai sab ko aazmaaya hum ne,
Ai Mehar, bani ka hai zamaana saathi,
Bigri ka koi yaar na paaya hum ne.

I perceive the face beloved in the meanest sod,
Everything displays the glory of my Lord,
He who saw the Creator in the created beings,
That seer, believe me, has had a glimpse of God.

Har shai mein jamaal-e-dilruba ko dekha,
Har cheez mein shaan-e-kibriya ko dekha,
Makhluq mein khaaliq nazr aaya jisko,
Us dekhne wale ne Khuda ko dekha.

سیّد احمد حُسین امّجد حیدرآبادی

ٹوٹا ہوا دل یادِ خدا کرتا ہے
عاشق ہی ادائے ناز پر مرتا ہے
رہتا ہے دلِ شکستہ میں عرش نشیں
یہ جام عجب ہے ٹوٹ کر بھرتا ہے

کب تک ہے بقائے تن فنا کو معلوم
کب تک ہے یہ زندگی قضا کو معلوم
ہر سانس یہ کہہ رہی ہے جاتے جاتے
جاتی تو ہوں واپسی خدا کو معلوم

تقدیر سے کیا گلا خدا کی مرضی
جو کچھ بھی ہوا، ہوا خدا کی مرضی
امجد ہر بات میں کہاں تک کیوں، کیوں،
ہر کیوں کی ہے انتہا، خدا کی مرضی

SAYED AHMED HUSSAIN AMJAD HYDERABADI (1878-1961)

A jilted heart to God doth tilt,
A lover by beauty's darts is killed;
Heaven abides in a broken heart,
Strange, when broken, this cup is filled.

Tuta hua dil yaad-e-Khuda karta hai,
Aashiq hi adaa-e-naaz par marta hai,
Rahta hai dil-e-shikasta mein arsh nashin,
Yeh jaam ajab hai ke toot kar bharta hai.

How long will this body last, death alone doth know,
Fate alone decides how long this life will go;
Every breath, as it expires, thus seems to say:
"God knows if I return, though, for sure, I go."

Kab tak hai baqaa-e-tan fana ko maalum,
Kab tak hai yeh zindagi qazaa ko maalum,
Har saans yeh kah rahi hai jaate jaate,
Jaati to hun, waapsi Khuda ko maalum.

Why quarrel with Fate, 'tis the will of God,
Whatever has happened is ordained by the Lord;
How long this insistence on the "why" of things?
Every "why" ends at last in the will of God.

Taqdeer se kya gila, Khuda ki marzi,
Jo kuchh bhi hua, hua Khuda ki marzi;
Amjad, har baat mein kahaantak kyon, kyon?
Har kyon ki intahaa, Khuda ki marzi.

امجد

کھیتی مرے فلسفہ کی پکتی ہی نہیں
تدبیر سے تقدیر چمکتی ہی نہیں
کھاتی ہے ہمیشہ منہ کی لیکن پھر بھی
یہ کیا، وہ کیوں، سے عقل تھکتی ہی نہیں

ہر ذرّہ پہ فضلِ کبریا ہوتا ہے
اِک چشمِ زدن میں کیا سے کیا ہوتا ہے
اصنام دبی زباں سے یہ کہتے ہیں
وہ چاہے تو پتھر بھی خدا ہوتا ہے

بیکس ہوں نہ مال ہے نہ سرمایہ ہے
مجھ سے کیا پوچھتا ہے کیا لایا ہے
یارب تری رحمت کے بھروسے، امجد
بند آنکھ کئے یوں ہی چلا آیا ہے

Amjad Hyderabadi

The crop of my philosophy is ever unripe,
Planning can never the writ of Fate unwrite;
Though rebuffed again and again, my reason, all the same;
With its "whats" and "whys", continues its fight.

Kheti mere phalsafe ki pakti hi nahin,
Tadbir se taqdeer chamakti he nahin,
Khaati hai hamesha munh ki lekin phir bhi,
"Yeh kya", "woh kyon," se aqal thakti hi nahin.

Every grain is blessed by the grace of God,
In the twinkling of an eye, what miracles are wrought!
In a suppressed voice, thus the idols say:
Aided by His will, a stone turns a god!

Har zarra pe fazal-e-kibriya hota hai,
Ik chashm-zadan mein kya se kya hota hai,
Asnaam, dabi zabaan se yeh kahte hain,
Woh chaahe to paththar bhi Khuda hota hai.

I'm utterly destitute, no wealth, no stock,
Embarrass me not by asking, "What have you brought?"
Banking on Thy mercy, Lord, Amjad has arrived,
Empty-handed, unequipped, without a care or thought.

Be-kas hun, na maal hai, na sarmaaya hai,
Mujh se kya puchhta hai, kya laaya hai?
Yaarab teri rahmat ke bharose, Amjad,
Band aankh kiye yun hi chala aaya hai.

امجدؔ

مرمر کے ، لحد میں میَں نے جا پائی ہے
یاں تک مجھے تیری ہی کشش لائی ہے
آ۔ اے میرے منہ چھپانے والے آجا
خلوت ہے ، شبِ تار ہے ، تنہائی ہے

دو دِل اک ہوں ، تو نخلِ جاں پھلتا ہے
دل گود میں حُسن و عشق کی پلتا ہے
سچ ہے کہ برقی روشنی کے مانند
دوتار سے زیست کا دیا جلتا ہے

بے فائدہ کب ہے جبّہ سائی اچّھی
طاعت میں نہیں خود نمُائی اچّھی
اِک سجدہ میں خاک کر دیا ہستی کو
حضرت تم سے دیا سلائی اچّھی

Amjad Hyderabadi

After a life-and-death struggle, I've found the grave,
Thy love alone my lord, has drawn me to this cave;
Come, my Love, why dost thou thus hide Thy face,
Dark night, utter seclusion—both lie in wait.

Mar mar ke, lahad mein main ne jaa paai hai,
Yaan tak mujhe teri hi kashish laai hai,
Aa, ai mere munh chhipaane waale aa jaa,
Khilwat hai, shab-e-taar hai, tanhaai hai.

When two hearts unite, a new life is born,
In the lap of love and beauty, the heart develops and
    warms;
As in electric light, so in real life,
By two wires conjoined, the flame of life is formed.

Do dil ik hon to nakhle-jaan phaltaa hai,
Dil gaud mein husn-o-ishq ki palta hai,
Such hai ke barqi roshni ki maanind,
Do taar se zeest ka diye jalta hai.

Why kneel and bend in an aimless way?
Self display is forbid when you sit and pray;
Just at one stroke it got itself dissolved,
A match-stick is better, sir, than your holy grace.

Be faayda kab hai jibba saai achchi,
Taait mein nahin khud-namaai achchi,
Ik sijda mein khaak kar diya hasti ko,
Hazrat tum se diya salaai achchi.

امجد

کوشش ہے تمام اپنی ستائش کیلئے
کیا کیا کرتے ہیں ایک خواہش کیلئے
ہر ایک نمود پر مِٹ جاتا ہے
پُتلے مٹّی کے ہیں نُمائش کیلئے

لے لے کے خُدا کا نام چلّاتے ہیں
پھر بھی اثرِ دُعا نہیں پاتے ہیں
کھاتے ہیں حرام لُقمہ، پڑھتے ہیں نماز
کرتے نہیں پرہیز، دوا کھاتے ہیں

سانچے میں اجل کے ہر گھڑی ڈھلتی ہے
ہر وقت یہ شمعِ زندگی ڈھلتی ہے
آتی جاتی ہے سانس اندر باہر
یا عُمر کے حلق پر چھُری چلتی ہے

Amjad Hyderabadi

All endeavour is aimed at winning fame and praise,
All of us strain and strive to satisfy this craze;
Every one is dying for vain-glorious show,
These models of clay are all for display.

Koshish hai tamaam apni sataaish ke lieye,
Kya kya karte hain ek khwahish ke lieye,
Har ek namud par mita jaata hai,
Putle mitti ke hain namaaish ke lieye.

Calling out the name of God they shout early and late,
Yet their loud prayers do not carry weight,
They eat the meal forbid, yet kneel and pray,
Though they take the medicine, precautions they but hate.

Le le ke Khuda ka naam chillaate hain,
Phir bhi asar-e-dua nahin paate hain,
Khaate hain haraam luqma, parhte hain namaaz,
Karte nahin parhez, dawa khaate hain.

Every hour has to pass through the mould of death,
Life's candle is melting down with each fleeting breath;
As I breathe in and out, I cannot but feel,
That a dagger sharp-edged is sawing off my neck.

Saanche mein ajal ke har ghari dhalti hai,
Har waqt ye shama-e-zindagi dhalti hai,
Aati jaati hai saans andar baahar,
Yaa, umr ke halq par chhuri chalti hai.

امجد

ہم صحبتِ بے خرد پریشان رہا
نا فہم کو سمجھا کے پشیمان رہا
تعلیم سے جاہل کی جہالت نہ گئی
نادان کو الٹا بھی تو نادان رہا

گیسو لہرا کے ناگ ہو جاتا ہے
نوحہ، آخر میں راگ ہو جاتا ہے
ہر چند دیا سلائی اِک تِنکا ہے
صرف ایک رگڑ سے آگ ہو جاتا ہے

پابندِ خیال میری تقریر رہی
آزادی پہ بھی پاؤں میں زنجیر رہی
تھا جتنا خدا کا حکم۔ کوشش کر لی
تدبیر بھی وابستۂ تقدیر رہی

Amjad Hyderabadi

A stupid man is a pain in the neck,
Counselling fools brings regret;
Education cannot a dunce improve,
A dud is a dud, even if reversed.

Hum suhbat-e-be khirad pareshaan raha,
Na faham ko samjha pashemaan raha,
Taalim se jaahal ki jahaalat na gai,
Naadaan ko ulta bhi to naadaan raha.

Locks of hair, set aflutter, serpentining grow,
A wail prolonged, in the end, becomes a song of woe;
A match-stick is seemingly a mere bit of straw,
Scratch it but once, it begins to glow.

Gaisu lahra ke naag ho jaataa hai,
Noha aakhir mein raag ho jaataa hai,
Har chand diya salaai ik tinka hai,
Siraf ik ragar se aag ho jaataa hai.

My speech has been a slave of thought,
Though free, our feet are fettered fast;
I have tried as much as God allowed,
Yet Fate controls our plans and plots.

Paaband-e-khayaal meri taqrir rahi,
Aazadi pe bhi paaon mein zanjeer rahi,
Tha jitna Khuda ka hukam koshish kar li,
Tadbir bhi waabasta-e-taqdeer rahi.

شوکت علی خاں فانیؔ بدایونی

کچھ خیر سے یادِ یار میں گذری عمر
کچھ موت کے انتظار میں گذری عمر
آیا بھی اگر ہوش تو بے چین رہے
کچھ نشے میں کچھ خمار میں گذری عمر

ہستی کے نہ آغاز نہ انجام میں دخل
تکلیف پہ قابو ہے نہ آرام میں دخل
اک سانس پہ عمر بھر بھی کبھی بس نہ چلا
مختار ہوں اَور نہیں کسی کام میں دخل

دُنیا کہیں دوزخ ہے، کہیں خُلدِ بریں
دل ہے وہی، ایک شاد ہے ایک حزیں
یہ ذرّہ چمک اُٹھا، وہ تاریک ہوا
جم کر نہ رہی شعاعِ خورشید کہیں

SHAUKAT ALI KHAN FANI BADAYUNI
(1879-1941)

Partly my life was spent thinking of my friend,
Partly it went away waiting for the end,
Even if I woke up, restless I remained,
Intoxication and hangover—thus my way did wend.

Kuchh khair se yaad-e-yaar mein guzri umr,
Kuchh maut ke intazaar mein guzri umr,
Aaya bhi agar hosh tau be-chain rahe,
Kuchh nashe mein kuchh khumaar mein guzri umr.

O'er our beginning or end, we've little control,
We must accept joy or pain as fate doth dole,
Not even a breath of life is subject to our will,
We are called sovereign, yet no power we hold.

Hasti ke na aaghaaz na anjaam mein dakhal,
Taklif pe qaabu hai, na aaraam mein dakhal,
Ik saans pe umr bhar bhi kabhi bas na chala,
Mukhtaar hun aur nahin kisi kaam mein dakhal.

Now the world is a paradise, now it's a hell,
Now the heart feels depressed, now with joy swells;
Here a grain is set aglow, there plunged in gloom,
Nowhere doth the sun's ray steadfastly dwell.

Duniya kahin dozakh hai, kahin khuld-e-barin,
Dil hai wohi, ek shaad hai ek hazin,
Yeh zarrah chamak utha, woh taarik hua,
Jam kar na rahi shuaa-e-khurshid kahin.

فانی

کیا خضرِ طریق کہہ کے رہزن کہتے
بنتی نہیں موم کہہ کے آہن کہتے
ورنہ وہ دوستوں نے ایذا دی ہے
شرم آتی ہے دُشمنوں کو دُشمن کہتے

بُجھتی ہی نہیں شمع ، جلے جاتی ہے
کٹتی ہی نہیں رات ، ڈھلے جاتی ہے
جاری ہے نفس کی آمد و شد فانی
سینے میں چھُری ہے کہ چلے جاتی ہے

کتنوں کو جگر کا زخم سہتے دیکھا
دیکھا ہے جسے خونِ دل ہی پیتے دیکھا
اب تک روتے تھے مرنے والوں کو اور اب
ہم رو دیئے جب کسی کو جیتے دیکھا

Fani

How can I call him a "robber" after I have called him "guide",
Can a thing be termed wax, then iron solidified?
Otherwise my friends have caused me such a pain,
That I feel ashamed to call my foes hostile.

Kya Khizar-e-tariq kah ke rahzan kahte,
Banti nahin mom kah ke aahan kahte,
Warna woh doston ne eezaa di hai,
Sharm aati hai dushmanon ko dushman kahte.

The taper doth not expire, but burns and burns,
The night doth not come to end, on its wheel it turns,
While the breath goes in and out, I seem to feel,
That a dagger in my breast to and fro doth run.

Bujhti hi nahin shama jale jaati hai,
Kat-ti hi nahin raat, dhale jaati hai,
Jaari hai nafas ki aamad-e-shud, Fani,
Seene mein chhuri hai ke chale jaati hai.

How many men have I seen nursing wounded hearts,
Or drinking their life-blood for the purple draught!
Formerly when someone died, we used to weep,
Now we weep when someone is seen to live and last.

Kitnon ko jigar ka zakhm sahte dekha,
Dekha jise khoon-e-dil hi peete dekha,
Ab tak roe the marne waalon ko, aur ab,
Hum ro dieye jab kisi ko jeete dekha.

فانی

محکوم ہیں حاکم کی حکومت کا شکار
کمزور زبردست کی قوت کا شکار
تھوڑی ہے جو ہو عورتوں پر سختی
جبتک ہیں یہ مَردوں کی جہالت کا شکار

دُکھ عورتوں کے سُنو زبانی اُن کی
سُننے ہی کے قابل ہے کہانی اُن کی
ٹیڑھے ہیں تو کون بَل نکالے اُن کے
سیدھے ہیں جو مرد مہربانی اُن کی

Fani

The subjects are subjected to the tyranny of the kings,
The weak are for the strong mere underlings,
No excess is too grave for the female race,
So long as the boorish male manipulates the strings.

Mahkoom hain haakim ki hakumat ka shikaar,
Kamzor zabardast ki quwwat ka shikaar,
Thori hai jo ho auraton par sakhti,
Jab tak hain yeh mardon ki jahaalat ka shikaar.

Let the women themselves narrate their tragic woes,
It deserves a hearing—their tale morose;
If the men are crooked, who can set them right?
If plain and simple, to them the credit goes.

Dukh auraton ke suno zabaani unki,
Sun-ne hi ke qaabil hai kahaani unki,
Terhe hain to kaun nikaale bal unke,
Seedhe hain jo mard, meharbaani unki.

یاس یگانہ چنگیزی

چارہ نہیں کوئی جلتے رہنے کے سوا
سانچے میں فنا کے ڈھلتے رہنے کے سوا
اے شمع تیری حیاتِ فانی کیا ہے
جھونکا کھانے، سنبھلتے رہنے کے سوا

مخمورِ مئے شباب ہو لینا تھا
کم سے کم ایک نیند سو لینا تھا
دامانِ ہوس کہیں بھگو لینا تھا
بہتی گنگا میں ہاتھ دھو لینا تھا

رونا ہے بدا جنھیں وہ جم جم روئیں
جب عیش مہیّا ہو تو ہم کیوں کھوئیں
فردا معلوم و رازِ فردا معلوم
رات اپنی ہے پھر کیوں نہ مزے سے سوئیں

YAAS YAGANA CHANGEZI
(1884-1956)

We cannot help but burn and burn,
In the mould of death to pine and yearn,
What else, O taper, is your life?
To cower and rise, turn by turn.

Chaaraa nahin koi jalte rahne ke siwaa,
Saanche mein fana ke dhalte rahne ke siwaa,
Ai shama, teri hayaat-e-faani kya hai,
Jhonka khaane, sambhalte rahne ke siwaa?

You should have let the wine of youth in your sinews
    seep,
You should have enjoyed at least one short spell of sleep,
You should have quenched the fire of your carnal needs,
You should have washed your hand in the Ganges deep.

Makhmoor-e-mai-e-shabaab ho lena tha,
Kam se kam ek neend so lena tha,
Daamaan-e-hawas kahin bhigo lena tha,
Bahti ganga mein haath dho lena tha.

Those prone to weep are welcome to weep,
When life abounds in joy, why miss the gala treat?
None can foresee the morrow, or its depths explore,
When we are given the night, why lose the bliss of sleep?

Rona hai bidaa jinhen woh jum jum roen,
Jab aish muhayya ho tau hum kyon khoen,
Farda maalum wa raaz-e-farda maalum,
Raat apni hai phir kyon na maze se soen.

یگانہ

ہوں صید کبھی اور کبھی صیّاد ہوں میں
کچھ بھی نہیں بازیچۂ اضداد ہوں میں
مختار مگر اپنی حدوں میں محدود
ہاں وُسعتِ زنجیر تک آزاد ہوں میں

کعبے کی طرف دُور سے سجدہ کروں
یا دَیر کا آخری نظارہ کروں
کچھ دیر کی مہمان ہے جاتی دُنیا
ایک اور گُنہ کروں یا توبہ کروں

مَردوں کا اصول جان لینے کی ہے دیر
دُشوار کو سہل جان لینے کی ہے دیر
منجھدار کیا ہے، آگ میں کود پڑوں
کچھ بھی نہیں دل میں ٹھان لینے کی ہی دیر

Yaas Yagana

Now I'm a hunter, now I'm a prey,
A wonder of contradictions is this being of clay;
Independent am I, but within the limits prescribed,
Beyond the length of my chain, I dare not stray.

Hun said kabhi aur kabhi sayyaad hun main,
Kuchh bhi nahin baazeecha-e-izdaad hun main,
Mukhtaar magar apni haddon mein mahdood,
Haan wusat-e-zanjeer tak aazad hun main.

Should I bow down to Kaaba, sitting thus afar,
Or, cast a parting glance on the idol-house ajar?
Evanescent is this flux of things,
Should I fall for another sin, or pledge no more to fall?

Kaabe ki taraf dur se sajda kar lun,
Yaa dair kaa aakhiri nazzaaraa kar lun,
Kuchh der ki mehmaan hai jaati duniya,
Ek aur gunaah kar lun, yaa tauba kar lun?

All you need is to learn the tenets of the brave,
Once you say, "Nothing is difficult!" nothing obstructs your way;
Not to talk about braving floods, I can plunge in fire,
All I need is a strong resolve not to be dismayed.

Mardon ka asool jaan lene ki hai der,
Dushwaar ko sahal jaan lene ki hai der,
Manjhdaar kya hai, aag mein kud parun,
Kuchh bhi nahin, dil mein thaan lene ki hai der.

کبھو رام جوش ملسیانی

ہر ایک کے دِل میں رکبرِ ہستی دیکھا
ہر ایک کے سر میں شورِ مستی دیکھا
پائی نہ کہیں خُدا پرستی ہم نے
ہر چیز میں رنگِ خود پرستی دیکھا

مُشکل کا یہ اصرار کہ اب کام نہ کر
مقصد کی یہ تاکید کہ آرام نہ کر
اُٹھ باندھ لے ہمّت کی کمر اے ناداں
آغاز کو شرمندۂ انجام نہ کر

تقدیر جب آبِ زر سے مُنہ دھوتی ہے
آلودہ وہ گردِ غم سے کب ہوتی ہے
زردار کے گھر میں رنج و غم ہنستے ہیں
نادار کے گھر میں خوشی روتی ہے

LABHU RAM JOSH MALSIANI
(1884-1976)

Every heart, we found, was stuffed with self-pride,
Every head was swollen with the wine of life,
We didn't find love of God anywhere on earth,
Self-love was the salient strand in everything we spied.

Har ek ke dil mein kibr-e-hasti dekha,
Har ek ke sar mein shor-e-masti dekha,
Paai na kahin Khuda parasti hum ne,
Har cheez mein rang-e-khud parasti dekha.

Obstacles daunt my will to work,
Duty will not let me shirk,
Up, up you fool, gird up your loins,
Let not your beginning your end besmirch.

Mushkil ka yeh israar ke ab kaam na kar,
Maqsad ki yeh taakid ke aaraam na kar,
Uth baandh le himmat ki kamar, ai nadaan,
Aaghaaz ko sharminda-e-anjaam na kar.

When in flowing gold Fate laves her face,
Dust of grief cannot slur her burnished grace,
Even the joys of the poor seem to wail and whine,
Sorrows start smiling, perched on an affluent face.

Taqdir jub aab-e-zar se munh dhoti hai,
Aaluda woh gard-e-ghum se kub hoti hai?
Zardaar ke ghar mein ranj-o-ghum hanste hain,
Nadaar ki duniya mein khushi roti hai.

جوش ملسیانی

آئی ہیں گھٹائیں تُو بھی آ اے ساقی
محفل کو سیہ مست بنا اے ساقی
ساغر کی ضرورت نہیں میخواروں کو
مستانہ نگاہوں سے پِلا اے ساقی

کچھ اپنی کرامت بھی دِکھا اَے ساقی
جو کھول دے آنکھیں وُہ پِلا اَے ساقی
ہشیار کو دیوانہ بنایا بھی تو کیا
دیوانے کو ہشیار بنا اَے ساقی

فانی ہی سہی یہ عُمر، باقی نہ سہی
پینے کی ہوس بھی خُوش مذاقی نہ سہی
تم گردنِ مینا کو جُھکا دو سرِ جام
محفل میں اگر نہیں ہے ساقی نہ سہی

144

Josh Malsiani

Now the clouds have come, Saqi, come without pretence,
Come, rob the gathering of their wit and sense;
The drinkers won't require the foaming cup of wine,
Enough is your drunken glance to throw them off the fence.

Aai hain ghataaen tu bhi aa, ai Saqi,
Mehfal ko seaah mast bana, ai Saqi,
Saaghar ki zaroorat nahin hai maikhwaaron ko,
Mastana nigaahon se pila, ai Saqi.

Some of your miraculous might you should now expose,
Serve us thou, O Saqi, with the eye-awakening dose;
Turning saner folks mad is no act of grace,
Shaking off the frenzy's stupor, this your magic shows.

Kuchh apni karamat bhi dikha, ai Saqi,
Jo khol de aankhen wo pila, ai Saqi,
Hushiar ko diwaana banaaya bhi tau kya,
Diwaane ko hushiar bana, ai Saqi.

Granted that life's mortal, it won't for aye stay,
Wine-bibbing, let's admit, cannot win us praise;
Bend thou, all the same, the flask into the cup,
What matters if Saqi the gathering doesn't grace.

Fani hi sahi yeh umr, baqi na sahi,
Peene ki hawas bhi khush mazaaqi na sahi;
Tum gardan-e-meena ko jhuka do sar-e-jaam,
Mehfil mein agar nahin hai saqi, na sahi.

تلوک چند محروم

دروازہ نجات کا بیاباں میں نہیں
دل کا آرام قصر و ایوان میں نہیں
تسکین جنّت میں بھی نہیں مل سکتی
جب تک موجود قلبِ انساں میں نہیں

دُنیا نے عجب رنگ جما رکھّا ہے
ہر اک کو غلام اپنا بنا رکھّا ہے
پھر لُطف یہ ہے کہ جس سے پوچھو وُہ کہے
اِس عالمِ آب و گِل میں کیا رکھّا ہے

طِفلی تھی وقف ناز و نعمت کے لیے
تھا عہدِ شباب خوابِ غفلت کے لیے
پیری ہوئی نذرِ ضُعفِ پیری، افسوس!
رکھا تھا جسے مَیں نے ریاضت کے لیے!

146

TILOK CHAND MEHROOM
(1887-1965)

The abode of eternal bliss is not in lonesome wilds,
Nor in palace royal inner peace abides;
You cannot find peace of mind even in Paradise,
Unless this element your own heart provides.

Darwaaza nijaat ka bayabaan mein nahin,
Dil ka aaraam qasar-o-aiwaan mein nahin;
Taskin jannat mein bhi nahin mil sakti,
Jab tak maujood qalab-e-insaan mein nahin.

What a spell this world has cast,
All submit to the world at last;
Yet, how surprising, all should say,
This mundane place tempts us not.

Duniya ne ajab rung jama rakhkha hai,
Har ik ko ghulaam apna bana rakhkha hai;
Phir lutaf yeh ke jis se puchho woh kahe,
Is aalam-e-aab-o-gil mein kya rakhkha hai?

By comforts and caresses was childhood teased,
Youth was spent in dreamful ease,
Old age, reserved for toil and work,
Was, alas! senility-seized.

Tifli thi waqaf-e-naaz-o-neimat ke lieye,
Tha ahd-e-shabaab khwaab-e-ghaflat ke lieye,
Peeri hui nazr-e-zof-e-peeri, afsos!
Rakhkha tha jise main ne riaazat ke lieye.

محروم

اے روشنیٔ شعور دینے والے
ذرّوں کو ضیائے طُور دینے والے
دیدار طلب ہے چشمِ حیراں میری
اے شمس و قمر کو نُور دینے والے

اُٹھتی ہی نہیں نظر، جُھکی جاتی ہے
نادم ہے، خاک پر جُھکی جاتی ہے
سر پر ہے عمر بھر کا بارِ عصیاں
پیری میں جو یُوں کمر جُھکی جاتی ہے

ہم بُھول کو اپنی علم و فن سمجھے ہیں
غُربت کے مقام کو وطن سمجھے ہیں
منزل پہ پہنچ کے جھاڑ دیں گے اِسکو
یہ گردِ سفر ہے جس کو تن سمجھے ہیں

148

Mehroom

O Thou the radiant Reason's mine,
Which floods the earth with effulgence divine,
My bewildered eyes crave Thy glimpse,
Thy light in sun and moon doth shine.

Ai roshani-e-shaoor dene waale,
Zarron ko zayaa-e-Tur dene waale,
Deedaar-talab hai chashme-hairaan meri,
Ai shams-o-qamar ko noor dene waale.

I durst not raise my eyes, down bends my brow,
Weighed down by shame, they graze the dust below,
A life-time of sins bows down the head,
That's why in old age, the back becomes a bow.

Uthti hi nahin nazr, jhuki jaati hai,
Naadim hai, khaak par jhuki jaati hai,
Sar par hai umr bhar ka baar-e-isiaan,
Peeri mein jo yun qamar jhuki jaati hai.

We confuse our errors with learning and lore,
For our native land, mistake the alien shore,
We'll shake it off when we reach the goal,
What we call our body, is way-side dust—no more.

Hum bhool ko apni ilam-o-fun samjhe hain,
Ghurbat ke maqaam ko watan samjhe hain,
Manzil pe pauhnch ke jhaar denge isko,
Yeh gard-e-safar hai jisko tun samjhe hain.

محروم

کوئی ہے تمنّائے زر و مال میں خوش
کوئی ہے تماشائے خط و خال میں خوش
بیدلؔ سب کو بہ حالِ ابتر دیکھا
خوشحال وُہی ہے جو ہے ہر حال میں خوش

آئینۂ دل کو گردِ کیں سے رکھ صاف
کر دے اہلِ ریا کے کینوں کو معاف
دُنیا میں نہ کر کسی سے بے انصافی
دُنیا سے مگر نہ رکھ اُمّیدِ انصاف

پرّاں شام سحر ہُوتے جاتے ہیں
ایّام یُوں ہی بسر ہُوتے جاتے ہیں
جبسے ہُوئے دُور ہم سے مرنیو الے
ہم اُن سے قریب تر ہُوتے جاتے ہیں

Mehroom

Some find joy in wealth and state,
Some are charmed by a beauteous face,
But all are found to be ill-at-ease,
Except those content in every state.

Koi hai tamannaa-e-zar-o-maal mein khush,
Koi hai tamaashaa-e-khat-o-khaal mein khush,
Bedil sab ko ba-haal-e-abtar dekha,
Khushhaal wohi hai jo hai har haal mein khush.

Let not malice mulch the mirror of your heart,
Forgive the cunning folks for their venomous darts,
Be thou just and fair to the world at large,
Expect thou no justice on the world's part.

Aaeena-e-dil ko gard-e-keen se rakh saaf,
Kar de ahl-e-riyaa ke keenon ko maaf,
Duniya mein na kar kisi se be insaafi,
Duniya se magar na rakh umeed-e-insaaf.

Days and nights are fleeting fast,
Life is slipping away unthought,
Day by day we are closing on
Our friends, long removed and lost.

Parraan shaam sahar hue jaate hain,
Ayyaam yunhi basar hue jaate hain,
Jab se hue door hum se marne waale,
Hum un se qarib tar hue jaate hain.

جگت موہن لال روآں

کَیسی آخر یہ بزمِ نُورانی ہے
کِس کے جلوؤں کی یہ فراوانی ہے
یہ ماہِ دو ہفتہ اَور یہ صبحِ جمیل
کِس کا رُخسار، کِس کی پیشانی ہے

اپنے ساقی سے کل یہ پُوچھا مَیں نے
کِتنے میخوار تشنہ لب آتے ہیں
بولا کہ مقدّرات ہیں ساغر و مے
آنے کی اگر کہو تو سب آتے ہیں

وُہ لذّتِ شورشِ نہانی نہ رہی
وُہ ذوقِ طلب وُہ جانفشانی نہ رہی
جینا نہیں نام سانس لینے کا روآں
کیا لُطفِ حیات جب جوانی نہ رہی

JAGAT MOHAN LAL RAWAN
(1889-1934)

How glorious is this world, in fact,
Whose grace divine permeates this tract?
This rounded moon, this beauteous morn,
Whose cheeks, whose forehead reflect?

Kaisi aakhir yeh bazm-e-nooraani hai,
Kis ke jalwon ki yeh farawaani hai,
Yeh maah-e-do haftah, aur yeh subah-e-jameel,
Kis ka rukhsaar, kis ki peshaani hai?

I asked my Saqi yesterday,
How many drinkers arrive athirst;
Fate, he said, allots the wine and glass,
Though one and all into the tavern burst.

Apne Saqi se kal yeh puchha main ne,
Kitne maikhwaar tishna lab aate hain,
Bola ke muqaddaraat hain saagar-o-mai,
Aane ki agar kaho to sab aate hain.

Gone the thrill of inner turmoil,
The questing zeal, the honest toil,
Life is not breathing, Rawan,
When youth departs, life's despoiled.

Woh lazzat-e-shorash-e-nihaani na rahi,
Woh zauq-e-talab woh jaanfishaani na rahi,
Jeena nahin naam saans lene ka Rawan,
Kya lutaf-e-hayaat jub jawaani na rahi.

روآں

حرصِ و ہوسِ حیاتِ فانی نہ گئی
اس دل سے امیدِ کامرانی نہ گئی
ہے سنگِ مزار پر تیرا نام روآں
مَر کر بھی امّیدِ زندگانی نہ گئی

کیا تم سے بتائیں عمرِ فانی کیا تھی
بچپن کیا چیز تھا، جوانی کیا تھی
یہ گُل کی مہک تھی، وہ ہوا کا جھونکا
اِک موجِ فنا تھی، زندگانی کیا تھی

نوروز ہے غرقِ بادہ دُنیا کر دے
میرا ارمان آج پُورا کر دے
پی لوں میں شراب بھر کے اِسمیں ساقی
تُو کاسۂ آسمان کو سیدھا کر دے

Rawan

Thirst for mortal life persists,
Desire for name and fame subsists,
The grave-stone displays your name, Rawan,
Though dead, the hope of life exists.

Hiras-o-hawas-e-hayaat-e-faani na gai,
Is dil se umeed-e-kaamraani na gai,
Hai sung-e-mazaar par tera naam, Rawan,
Mar kar bhi umeed-e-zindagaani na gai.

What was mortal life? What should I say?
What was childhood, what the youth's hey day?
One was the whiff of breeze, the other floral scent,
Life was, in short, a death-delivering wave.

Kya tum se bataaen umr-e-faani kya thi,
Bachpan kya cheez tha, jawaani kya thi,
Yeh gul ki mahak thi, woh hawa ka jhonka,
Ik mauj-e-fana thi, zindagaani kya thi.

Drown the world in wine, 'tis New Year day,
O, let me have my fill just for today;
Turn upright this skiey bowl, so that I may,
Fill it to the brink, and drink it all away.

Nau roz hai gharaq-e-baada duniya kar de,
Mera armaan aaj poora kar de,
Pee loon main sharaab bhar ke is mein Saqi,
Tu kaasaa-e-aasmaan ko seedha kar de.

رواں

تابع ہمیں عقل کا کئے دیتی ہے
آزادیٔ دلِ فن کئے دیتی ہے
تہذیب کی عظمتوں سے باز آئے ہم
فطرت سے ہمیں جُدا کئے دیتی ہے

کل صبح نے مُسکرا کے تاروں سے کہا
ہو جائیں گے اب تمہارے انوار فنا
تاروں نے کہا کہ ہم رہیں گے یوں ہی
تُو آئے گی اور ختم ہو جائے گی، آ

کچھ وقت اگر خوشی میں کٹ جاتا ہے
تسکین ہوتی ہے، رنج بٹ جاتا ہے
اکثر تو کچھ ایسا حال ہوتا ہے رواں
بالکل دُنیا سے جی اُچٹ جاتا ہے

Rawan

It binds us with the Reason's strings,
It tends to clip the heart's wings;
The march of civilization leaves us cold,
With mother nature it breaks our links.

Taabe hamen aqal ka kieye deti hai,
Aazaadi-e-dil fana kieye deti hai,
Tahzib ki azmaton se baaz aae hum,
Fitrat se hamen juda kieye deti hai.

Smilingly the morn thus addressed the stars:
Your sparkling brilliance will soon get dissolved;
The stars made reply; we will not change at all,
'Tis you who will vanish, come, meet your fall.

Kal subah ne muskra ke taaron se kaha,
Ho jaaen ge ab tumhaare unwaar fana,
Taaron ne kaha ke hum rahenge yunhi,
Tu aaegi aur khatam ho jaaegi, aa!

If some moments of joy fall into my lap,
I can loosen my heart, I can then relax;
But oft times, Rawan, I feel so bad,
Weary seems this life, the world nothing but trash.

Kuchh waqt agar khushi mein kat jaata hai,
Taskin hoti hai, ranj bat jaataa hai,
Aksar to kuchh aisa haal hota hai, Rawan,
Bilkul duniya se ji uchat jaataa hai.

رواں

آزاد ضمیر ہو، فقیری یہ ہے
دل بے پروا رہے، امیری یہ ہے
زنجیر نہیں باعثِ قید، رواں
محدود رہے خیال، اسیری یہ ہے

انسان معذور، فکرِ انسان معذور
یہ کس کو خبر کہ کیا ہے اُس کو منظور
پیمانہ بدست رِند اَور اُسکے قریب
تسبیح بدست واعظ اَور اُس سے دُور

Rawan

You are a very saint, if your mind is free,
If you have a carefree heart, you are rich, indeed;
Chains cannot, Rawan, enslave a man,
If your thought is fettered, you lose your liberty.

Aazaad zameer ho, faqiri yeh hai,
Dil beparwaah rahe, ameeri yeh hai,
Zanjeer nahin baais-e-qaid, Rawan,
Mahdud rahe khayaal, aseeri yeh hai.

Powerless is man, powerless, too, his mind,
Who knows what He desires of the human kind!
A cup-weilding reveller, and so near His heart!
A priest telling beads—left far behind!

Insaan maazoor, fikr-e-insaan maazoor,
Yeh kis ko khabar ke kya hai usko manzoor,
Paimaana ba dast rind aur uske qarib,
Tasbih ba dast waaiz aur us se door.

رگھوپتی سہائے فراق گورکھپوری

جُز میرے یہ رنگِ حُسن اُچھالے کس نے
سانچے میں یہ خط و خال ڈھالے کس نے
سازِ بے نغمہ تھا یہ جسم رنگیں
اِس ساز سے یہ بول نکالے کس نے

غُنچے کو نسیم گُدگُدائے جیسے
مُطرب کوئی ساز چھیڑ جائے جیسے
یُوں پھوٹ رہی ہے مُسکراہٹ کی کرن
مندر میں چراغ جھلملائے جیسے

لہروں میں کھلا کمل نہاتے جیسے
دوشیزۂ صُبح گنگنائے جیسے
یہ رُوپ، یہ لوچ، یہ ترنّم، یہ نِکھار
بچّہ سوتے میں مُسکرائے جیسے

RAGHUPATI SAHAI FIRAQ GORAKHPURI (1896-1982)

Who but I did highlight the beauty's form and grace?
Who but I did mould the lineaments of the face?
Muted lay the organ of the sensuous frame,
Who awakened the melody slumbering in the cage?

Juz mere yeh rang-e-husn uchhaale kis ne,
Saanche mein yeh khat-o-khaal dhaale kis ne,
Saaz-e-benaghma tha yeh jisam-e-rangeen,
Is saaz se yeh bol nikaale kis ne.

Like the bud tickled by the breeze,
Or the strings by a musician teased,
Thus springs her radiant smile,
As a lamp aglimmer at the temple's feet.

Ghunche ko naseem gudgudaai jaise,
Mutrib koi saaz chher jaae jaise,
Yoon phoot rahi hai muskuraahat ki kiran,
Mandir mein chiragh jhilmalaae jaise.

Like a blooming lotus, water-steeped,
Like the Maid of Morn murmuring sweet,
Such beauty, such brightness, such melody, such grace,
Like a tender bade asmile in sleep.

Lahron mein khila kamal nahaae jaise,
Dosheezaa-e-subah gungunaae jaise,
Yeh roop, yeh loch, yeh tarannun, yeh nikhaar,
Bachcha sote mein muskuraae jaise.

فراق

اے معنیِ کائنات مُجھ میں آجا
اے رازِ صفات و ذات مُجھ میں آجا
سوتا ہے سنسار جھلملاتے تارے
اب بھیگ چلی ہے رات مُجھ میں آجا

جب تاروں نے جگمگاتے نیزے تولے
جب شبنم نے فلک سے موتی رولے
کچھ سوچ کے خلوت میں بصد ناز اُسنے
نرم اُنگلیوں سے بند قبا کے کھولے

واعظ تیری جنّت ہے فقط وہم و گُماں
ہے رُوکشِ فردوسِ بریں باغِ جہاں
تُو اِس کو فریبِ رنگ و بُو کہتا ہے
تِنکا بھی ہے اِس باغ کا رشکِ رگِ جاں

Firaq Gorakhpuri

O spirit of the universe, descend unto me,
O secret of Being and Virtue, descend unto me,
The world slumbers, the stars glimmer,
Rich and ripe grows the night, descend Thou to me!

Ai maani-e-kaaenaat mujh mein aa jaa,
Ai raaz-e-sifaat-e-zaat mujh mein aa jaa,
Sotaa sansaar, jhilmalaate taare,
Ab bhig chali hai raat, mujh mein aa jaa.

When stars their shining spears did hold,
When dew its gems from heavens rolled,
With winsome wiles, seclusion-sheltered, stirred by some
    thought,
She plied her delicate fingers, and undid her robe.

Jab taaron ne jagmagaate neze tole,
Jab shabnam ne falak se moti role,
Kuchh soch ke khilwat mein basad naaz usne,
Naram unglion se bund qibaa ke khole.

Your heaven, O priest, is a myth and a lie,
Envy of elysium is earthly paradise,
Mirage-like appears to you this world of scent and hue,
For me even a blade of grass vibrates with life.

Waaiz teri jannat hai faqat waham-o-gumaan,
Hai ru-kash-e-firdaus-e-barin bagh-e-jahaan,
Tu isko fareb-e-rang-o-boo kahta hai,
Tinka bhi hai is bagh kaa rashk-e-rag-e-jaan.

فراق

حمّام میں عُریانیٔ تن کا عالَم
پیکر کا دُھندلکے میں جھلکنا کم کم
ایک ہلکی تھرتھری سی سر سے پا تک
شبنم سے دُھلی شفق بھی کھاتی ہے قسم

افلاک پہ جب پرچمِ شب لہرایا
ساقی نے بھرا ساغرِ مَے چھلکایا
کچھ سوچ کے پچھ دیر تامّل کر کے
اُس نے بھی ذرا پردۂ رُخ سرکایا

مے خانے نے انقلاب کتنے دیکھے
کتنے جُگ آئے اور مٹّی میں مِلے
کتنا مُشکل ہے، کتنے سُورج سرِ جام
ساقی، اُبھرے، چڑھے، ڈھلے اور ڈُوبے

164

Firaq Gorakhpuri

O that beauty nude, in the bath algeam!
A shimmering shape, twilight draped, more glimpsed
    than seen,
A gentle shiver from head to heel—such state, such sight!
Even the flush of dewy dawn swears by this scene.

Hamaam mein uriaani-e-tun kaa aalam,
Paikar kaa dhundalke mein jhalakna kum, kum,
Ek halki tharthari si sar se paa tak,
Shabnam se dhuli shafaq bhi khaati hai qasam.

When the flag of night fluttered in the sky,
The Saqi shook the brimming cup with great delight,
Thinking for a moment, waiting for a while,
She too pushed her veil from her face aside.

Aflaak pe jab parcham-e-shab lahraaya,
Saqi ne bhara saghar-e-mai chhalkaaya,
Kuchh soch ke, kuchh der taaummal karke,
Us ne bhi zara parda-e-rukh sarkaaya.

Many a revolution the tavern has witnessed,
Many an age sprang to sight and vanished in the dust;
Who can count, Saqi, the innumerable suns,
That rose and flashed over the cup, then sank and set.

Maikhaane ne inqalaab kitne dekhe,
Kitne jug aai aur mitti mein mile,
Ginana mushkil hai kitne suraj sar-e-jaam,
Saqi, ubhre, charhe, dhale aur doobe.

فراق

صحرا میں زمان و مکاں کے کھو جاتی ہیں
صدیوں بیدار رہ کے سو جاتی ہیں
اکثر سوچا کیا ہوں خلوت میں ، فراق
تہذیبیں کیوں غروب ہو جاتی ہیں

ہر عیب سے مانا کہ جُدا ہو جائے
کیا ہے اگر انسان خُدا ہو جائے
شاعر کا تو بس کام ہے یہ ، ہر دل میں
کچھ دردِ حیات سِوا ہو جائے

اس راز سے کر رہا ہوں تجھ کو آگاہ
ممنوع و حرام کچھ نہیں ہے واللہ
جس کام میں محویّتِ کامل نہ رہے
اے دوست سمجھ لے کہ ہے وُہ کام گُناہ

Firaq Gorakhpuri

Sands of time drive them under,
They wake for centuries, then they slumber,
Why civilisations decay and die—
When alone, I muse and wonder.

Sahraa mein zamaan-o-makaan ke kho jaati hain,
Sadion bedaar rah ke so jaati hain,
Aksar socha kiya hun khilwat mein Faraq,
Tahziben kyon gharub ho jaati hain.

Assume that he eschews his faults,
What, if man becomes a god?
The poet is guided by one aim:
To create compassion in every heart.

Har aib se maana ke juda ho jaae,
Kya hai agar insaan Khuda ho jaae,
Shaair ka to bus kaam hai yeh, har dil mein,
Kuchh dard-e-hayaat siwa ho jaae.

This secret to you, lo, I impart,
Nothing is forbidden, nothing is barred,
But where your heart is not involved,
There the guilt resides, there the sin resorts.

Is raaz se kar raha hun tujhko aagaah,
Mamnu-o-haraam kuchh nahin, wallah,
Jis kaam mein mahwiat-e-kaamal na rahe,
Ai dost, samajh le ke hai woh kaam gunaah.

فراق

مے کا ہر نیم قطرہ ہے آفتِ جاں
نشے سے بڑے بڑوں نے مانگی ہے اماں
یہ وزن کا معجزہ ہے طُرفہ ساقی
انگور کی پنکھڑی پہاڑوں سی گراں

تنہائی میں ہم کس کو بُلائیں اَے دوست
تم دُور رہو کس کے پاس جائیں اَے دوست
اِس دولتِ فرُصت سے تو دم گھُٹتا ہے
یہ نقدِ شب کہاں بھُنائیں اَے دوست

اَمرت وہ ہلاہل کو بنا دیتی ہے
غصّے کی نظر پھُول کھلا دیتی ہے
ماں لاڈی اولاد کو جیسے تارے
کس پیار سے پریمی کو سزا دیتی ہے

Firaq Gorakhpuri

Each droplet of wine is the bane of life,
"Save us, God, from wine," even the great do cry;
It's indeed, Saqi, a great miracle of weight,
A vineleaf is heavier far than the mountain high!

Mai ka har neem qatra hai aafat-e-jaan,
Nashe se bare baron ne maangi hai amaan,
Yeh wazan ka mojza hai turfa, Saqi,
Angoor ki pankhari pahaaron se giraan.

Whom should I call, O friend, in my lonely state,
Where should I look for help, you aren't near, my mate;
This glut of time weighs on my nerves,
This bond of endless night, who will liquidate?

Tanhaai mein hum kis ko bulaaen, ai dost,
Tum dur ho kis ke paas jaaen, ai dost,
Is daulat-e-fursat se to dam ghut-ta hai,
Yeh naqad-e-shab kahaan bhunaaen, ai dost.

From poison she can nectar churn,
Flower-like her frown doth spurn,
As a mother chides her child,
She scolds her lover with fond concern.

Amrit woh halahal ko bana deti hai,
Ghusse ki nazar phool khila deti hai;
Maan laadli aulaad ko jaise taare,
Kis payaar se premi ko sazaa deti hai.

فراق

بہت پہلے سے اِن قدموں کی آہٹ جان لیتے ہیں
تجھے اَے زندگی ہم دُور سے پہچان لیتے ہیں
طبیعت اپنی گھبراتی ہے جب سُنسان راتوں میں
تو ایسے میں تِری یادوں کی چادر تان لیتے ہیں

تُو ہاتھ کو جب ہاتھ میں لے لیتی ہے
دُکھ درد زمانے کے مِٹا دیتی ہے
سنسار کے اِس تپتے ہوئے ویرانے میں
سُکھ شانت کی گویا تُو ہری کھیتی ہے

آغوشِ مُلائم میں سُلایا ہم کو
خاموش آواز سے جگایا ہم کو
کچھ ہم بھی بنائیں تیرے بگڑے ہوئے کام
اَے خاکِ وطن تُو نے بنایا ہم کو

Firaq Gorakhpuri

I can hear your footfalls long before you call,
I can make you out, my life, even from afar,
When on lonesome nights fear grips my heart,
The coverlet of your memory provides a safe resort.

Bahut pahle se in qadmon ki aahat jaan lete hain,
Tujhe, ai zindagi, hum dur se pahchaan lete hain;
Tabiat apni ghabraati hai jab sunsaan raaton mein,
To aise mein teri yaadon ki chaadar taan lete hain.

When, my Love, you hold my hand,
Hordes of sorrows you disband;
In this world's burning wild,
Green, oasis-like you stand.

Tu haath ko jab haath mein le leti hai,
Dukh dard zamaane ke mita deti hai;
Sansaar ke is tapte hue weeraane mein,
Sukh shaant ki goya tu hari kheti hai.

In your soft lap you cuddled us to sleep,
With your silences you broke our slumbers deep,
Let us too, O Motherland, alleviate your ills,
Your soil has moulded the face and form we keep.

Aaghosh-e-mulaayam mein sulaaya hum ko,
Khaamosh aawaaz se jagaaya hum ko,
Kuchh hum bhi banaain tere bigre hue kaam,
Ai khaak-e-watan tu ne banaaya hum ko.

شبّیر حسن خاں جوش ملیح آبادی

سُنو! اَے ساکنانِ بزمِ ہستی
نِدا کیا آرہی ہے آسماں سے
کہ آزادی کا اِک لمحہ ہے بہتر
غُلامی کی حیاتِ جاوداں سے

ہر سنگ میں شیشے کے مکاں ملتے ہیں
ہر تخم میں خُفتہ بوستاں ملتے ہیں
روندے ہُوئے ذرّوں کے لبوں پہ اَے جوش
خورشید کے بوسوں کے نِشاں ملتے ہیں

پستی میں بُلندی کا اشارہ گویا
کہرے میں ہے صُبح کا ستارہ گویا
اس کارگہِ فتنہ میں یُوں ہے شاعر
طوفان میں نُور کا مینارہ گویا

SHABBIR HASAN KHAN JOSH MALIHABADI (1898-1982)

O ye denizens of this earth,
Hark, what the heavens proclaim!
A single moment, freedom-crowned,
Outweighs eternal life in chains.

Suno ai saaknaan-e-bazam-e-hasti,
Nida kya aa rahi hai aasmaan se,
Ke aazaadi ka ik lamha hai behtar,
Ghulaami ki hayaat-e-jaavedaan se.

In every stone a glass-house sleeps,
In every seed a garden creeps,
From every trampled grain of dust,
A burning kiss of sunshine leaps.

Har sung mein sheeshe ke makaan milte hain,
Har tukham mein khufta bostaan milte hain,
Raunde hue zarron ke labon pe ai Josh,
Khurshid ke boson ke nishaan milte hain.

A promise of height in a world so low,
A phosphor bright in frost and snow,
In the sea of life, tempest-torn,
Beacon-like the poet doth glow.

Pasti mein bulandi ka ishaara goya,
Kuhre mein hai subah ka sitara goya;
Is kaar gahe fitna mein yun hai shaair,
Toofaan mein nur ka minaraa goya.

جوش

ہے صُبح اُفق سے جگمگانے والی
وعدے پہ ہے اُنکے مُسکرانے والی
جا پچھلے پہر کے چاند! اُن سے کہدے
اب رات ہے دو گھڑی میں جانیوالی

ہر غم، مئے گُل رنگ سے تھرّاتا ہے
آلامِ جہاں کا مُنہ اُتر جاتا ہے
لیکن جسے کہتے ہیں غمِ عشق اے جوشؔ
وُہ نشّے میں کچھ اور بھی بڑھ جاتا ہے

جب دل نے کُتب کو خضرِ راہ کیا
ہر حرف پہ غور، حسبِ دل خواہ کیا
تو اُن میں سے بیشتر کتابوں نے مُجھے
جہلِ اہلِ قلم سے آگاہ کیا

Josh Malihabadi

Soon the glimmering dawn will rise,
And mock her promise with a smile;
O dying moon, go tell my love:
The night shall die in a little while.

Hai subah ufaq se jagmagaane waali,
Waade pe hai unke muskuraane waali,
Jaa pichhle pahar ke chaand un se kah de:
Ab raat hai do ghari mein jaane waali.

All griefs submit to purple wine,
Worldly cares peak and pine,
But what we call the ache of love,
Stronger grows with draughts of wine.

Hur ghum mai-e-gul-rung se tharraata hai,
Aalaame-jahaan ka munh utar jaata hai,
Lekin jise kahte hain ghum-e-ishq, ai Josh,
Woh nashe mein kuchh aur bhi barh jaata hai.

When I turned to books in search of light,
And every word scrutinised,
In most of the books that I scanned,
The writers' ignorance sprang to sight.

Jab dil ne kutab ko Khizar-e-raah kiya,
Har haraf pe ghaur, hasb-e-dil khwaah kiya,
To un mein se beshtar kitaabon ne mujhe,
Jahal-e-ahl-e-qalam se aagaah kiya.

جوش

یہ رات گئے عینِ طرب کے ہنگام
پرتو یہ پڑا پُشت سے کِس کا سرِ جام؟
"یہ کون ہے"؟ "جبریل ہوں" "کیوں آئے ہو"
"سرکار! فلک کے نام کوئی پیغام"

کل رات گئے مست تھی جب موجِ نسیم
شبنم میں نہا رہی تھی پھولوں کی شمیم
اک حور نے ساغر سے نِکل کر یہ کہا
"میں رُوحِ مئے ہوش رُبا ہوں، تسلیم!"

کیا آج تعارف میں لجایا کوئی
کیا جانئے کیوں سنبھل نہ پایا کوئی
میں نے جو کہا "جوش مجھے کہتے ہیں"
آنکھوں کو جھُکا کے مُسکرایا کوئی

Josh Malihabadi

Late at night when I'm ecstasy-engrossed,
Whose reflection from behind in my cup is cast?
"Who art thou?" "Gabriel". "What brings you here?"
"Do you have, my Lord, a message for the gods?"

Yeh raat gaye aen tarab ke hangaam,
Partaw yeh para pusht se kis ka sar-e-jaam?
"Yeh kaun hai?" "Jibreel hun." "Kyon aae ho?"
"Sirkaar, falak ke naam koi paighaam?"

Late yesternight, when the drunken breeze blew,
When the floral fragrance bathed itself in dew,
A fairy rising from the flask thus spoke to me:
"I'm the spirit of maddening wine, good morn to you!"

Kal raat gaye mast thi jab mauj-e-naseem,
Shabnam mein naha rahi thi phoolon ki shamim,
Ik hoor ne saaghir se nikal kar yeh kaha:
"Main rooh-e-mai-e-hosh ruba hun, tasleem!"

As I introduced myself, why someone blushed and shied,
Why did she startle, why felt surprised?
When I said, "I am Josh," I don't know why,
Bending down her head, furtively she smiled.

Kya aaj taaruf mein lajaaya koi,
Kya jaaneye kyon sambhal na paaya koi,
Mein ne jo kaha, "Josh mujhe kahte hain,"
Aankhon ko jhuka ke muskraaya koi.

جوش

ہر سانس کو وقفِ صدشرارت کر دیں
اخلاق کی کچھ عجیب حالت کر دیں
مُفلس کہ امیروں کے گِناتے ہیں گُناہ
دولت اِنہیں دے دو تو قیامت کر دیں

ساقی کا بہر رنگ نظّارہ کروں
مَرتے مرتے بھی اِک اور اشارہ کروں
آدم کا یَیں ناخلف ہُوں فرزند اے جوش
عِصیاں سے اگر کبھی کنارہ کروں

ممکن ہے کہ اب جشنِ خرابات نہ ہو
اس رات کے بعد کوئی بھی رات نہ ہو
ٹھہرو کہ گلے تو مل لیں جانے والو
ممکن ہے کہ اب کبھی ملاقات نہ ہو

Josh Malihabadi

At every breath they 'uld devise mischiefs ever new,
Morality in their hands its own fate would rue,
The poor who blame the rich for their many faults,
Would bring the very doom on earth, if with wealth endued.

Har saans ko waqaf-e-sud sharaarat kar den,
Ikhlaaq ki kuchh ajib haalat kar den,
Muflis ke ameeron ke ginaate hain gunaah,
Daulat inhen de do to qayaamat kar den.

Let me gaze at Saqi in every form and state,
Let me cast another glance ere 'tis too late,
Unworthy son of Adam, Josh, I would prove to be,
If the life of sins I ever abdicate.

Saqi ka ba-har rung nazzaara kar loon,
Marte marte bhi ik aur ishaara kar loon,
Aadam ka mein naa khalf hun farzand, ai Josh,
Isiyaan se agar kabhi kinaara kar loon.

May be, we do not have another bacchic feast,
This may be the last night of our lively meet,
Pray, wait a while, let's have one parting embrace,
I fear that this may be our last chance to greet.

Mumkin hai ke ab jashan-e-kharaabaat na ho,
Is raat ke baad koi bhi raat na ho,
Thahro ke gale tau mil len jaane waalo,
Mumkin hai ke ab kabhi mulaaqaat na ho.

جوش

مرضی ہو تو سُولی پہ چڑھانا یا رب
یا نارِ جہنّم میں جلانا یا رب
معشوق کہیں آپ ہمارے ہیں بزرگ
ناچیز کو وُہ دِن نہ دِکھانا یا رب

کیا شیخ کی خشک زندگانی گُذری
بے چارے کی ایک شبِ سُہانی گُذری
دوزخ کے تخیل میں بُڑھاپا بیتا
جنّت کی دُعاؤں میں جوانی گُذری

چلنے میں ہیرے کی کنی رُلتی ہے
پلکوں کی ترازو میں حیا تُلتی ہے
جب کبھی ہوتے ہیں وُہ تبسّم فرما
غُنچے کی طرح دِل کی گرہ کھُلتی ہے

Josh Malihabadi

Hang me on the gallows, if you so desire,
Burn me if you like, O Lord, in infernal fire,
But let not this poor me live to see the day,
When sweethearts would remark: "You are our reverend sire."

Marzi ho tau sooli pe charhaana yaarab,
Ya naar-e-jahannam mein jalaana yaarab,
Maashuq kahen, aap hamaare hain bazurg,
Naa cheez ko woh din na dikhaana, yaarab.

How colourless was the preacher's life!
Poor man! for him no blissful night;
Fears of hell distressed his age,
His youth obsessed with paradise.

Kya sheikh ki khushk zindgaani guzri,
Bechaare ki ek shab na suhaani guzri,
Dozakh ke takhaiul mein burhapaa beeta,
Jannat ki duaaon mein jawaani guzri.

Her gait sparkling diamonds rolls,
The scale of eyelids coyness holds,
When sometimes she deigns to smile,
Bud-wise, my heart its knot unfolds.

Chalne mein heere ki kani rulti hai,
Palkon ki taraazu mein hayaa tulti hai,
Jab kabhi hote hain woh tabassum farma,
Ghunche ki tarah dil ki girah khulti hai.

جوش

شانوں پہ ہے چھٹکی ہوئی زلفوں کی لٹک
اعضا میں ہے تازہ شاخِ گُل کی سی لچک
اور اُس پہ یہ انگڑائی کا عالَم کہ نہ پوچھ
بِکھری ہوئی بدلیوں میں جس طرح دھنک

جس وقت جھلکتی ہے مناظر کی جبیں
راسخ ہوتا ہے ذاتِ باری کا یقیں
کرتا ہوں جب اِنساں کی تباہی پہ نظر
دل پوچھنے لگتا ہے، خُدا ہے کہ نہیں

دِل کو کوئی ضربِ غم سے کس طرح بچائے
جب کھُل کے ہنسے، آنکھوں میں آنسو بھر آئے
دیکھا کہ جہاں بھی ہے چراغاں کی بہار
بیٹھے ہیں وہیں پالتی مارے ہوئے سائے

Josh Malihabadi

Cascades of locks on shoulders lie,
Like a floral branch the limbs are lithe,
On top that yawn beyond compare!
A rainbow bent over cloudlets high!

Shaanon pe hai chhatki hui zulfon ki latak,
Aazaa mein hai taaza shaakh-e-gul ki si lachak,
Aur us pe yeh angraai ka aalam ke na puchh.
Bikhri hui badlion mein jis tarah dhanak.

When the sights of nature glimmer before my eyes,
My faith in God gets fortified,
But when I think of man and his heinous deeds,
"Doth God exist?" I ask mystified.

Jis waqt jhalkti hai manaazar ki jabeen,
Raasikh hota hai zaat-e-baari ka yaqeen,
Karta hun jab insaan ki tabaahi par nazar,
Dil puchhne lagta hai, Khuda hai ke nahin.

How can you save your heart from the blows of grief,
When the heart brims with laughter, eyes begin to weep,
Wherever glimmers a row of lamps, there you also find,
A swarm of shadows, squatting underneath.

Dil ko koi zarb-e-ghum se kistarah bachaae,
Jab khul ke hanse, aankh mein aansu bhar aae,
Dekha ke jahaan bhi hai chiraaghaan ki bahaar,
Baithe hain wahin paalti maare hue saae.

جوش

کل رات کیا جوش میں آیا ساقی
میرے شیون پہ گنگنایا ساقی
میں نے جو کہا مقصدِ ہستی کیا ہے
ساغر چھلکا کے مسکرایا ساقی

محشر میں پہنا رہے ہیں مجھ کو زنجیر
اِک بندۂ مجبور کی آخر تقصیر
آواز تو دو کوئی، کدھر ہیں آخر
ماحول و وِراثت و سرشت و تقدیر

مرنے پہ نویدِ جاں ملے یا نہ ملے
یہ کنج، یہ بوستاں ملے یا نہ ملے
پینے میں کسر نہ چھوڑ او خانہ خراب
معلوم نہیں وہاں ملے یا نہ ملے

Josh Malihabadi

How flushed, indeed, was Saqi yesternight,
As I sat complaining he hummed with delight;
When I asked in earnest: what's the aim of life?
He shook his flask in style, and gave a subtle smile.

Kal raat kya josh mein aaya, Saqi,
Mere shaiwan pe gungunaaya, Saqi,
Main ne jo kaha maqsad-e-hasti kya hai,
Saghar chhalka ke muskraaya Saqi.

On the day of Reckoning I am being enchained,
What for, after all, is this helpless man arraigned?
Answer please someone, what allowance is made,
For environs and inheritance, nature, fate ordained?

Mahshar mein pahna rahe hain mujhko zanjeer,
Ik banda-e-majboor ki aakhir taqseer?
Aawaaz tau do koi, kidhar hain aakhir,
Maahaul-o-wiraasat-o-sarishat-o-taqdeer?

Another life after death, we may or mayn't get,
This retreat, this garden seat, we may or mayn't get,
Drink without a stint, O thou luckless man,
Who knows in the world beyond we may or mayn't get.

Marne pe naweed-e-jaan mile ya na mile,
Yeh kunj, yeh bostaan, mile ya na mile,
Peene mein kasar na chhor, O khaana kharaab,
Maalum nahin waan mile ya na mile.

جوش

وہ کُفر کی تکرار کئے جاتا ہے
یہ دین یہ اصرار کئے جاتا ہے
اِک عُمر سے اِنکار پہ مائل ہے دماغ
اور دل ہے کہ اقرار کئے جاتا ہے

اِک ذرّہ ناچیز کو انجُم سمجھا
اِک مَوجِ خفیف کو تلاطُم سمجھا
اِس علمِ قلیل کو کہ ہے صرف اِک بُوند
افسوس کہ جاہلوں نے قُلزم سمجھا

کیا جانئے چہرہ زرد ہوتا کیوں ہے
دِل رنج و الم سے پُر ہوتا کیوں ہے
افسوس کہ اِتنا بھی نہیں معلوم
کانٹا چُبھنے سے درد ہوتا کیوں ہے

Josh Malihabadi

One proclaims atheistic creed,
The other affirms strong belief,
Life long "nay" is the head's refrain,
Eternal "yea" the heart repeats.

Woh kufar ki takraar kiye jaata hai,
Yeh deen pe israar kiye jaata hai,
Ik umr se inkaar pe maayal hai dimaagh,
Aur dil hai ke iqraar kiye jaata hai.

A tiny speck is deemed a star,
A ripple confused with tempest large,
A little knowledge, no more than a drop,
By the ignorant, alas, is ocean called.

Ik zarra-e-naa cheez ko anjum samjha,
Ik mauj-e-khafif ko talaatum samjha,
Is ilam-e-qalil ko ke hai sirafik boond,
Afsos ke jaahalon ne qulzum samjha.

We know not why the face grows pale,
Or why the heart with grief doth wail,
Alas, we even do not know,
Why the prick of a thorn pain entails.

Kya jaaneye chehra zard hota kyon hai,
Dil ranjo-o-alam se pur hota kyon hai,
Afsos ke itna bhi nahin maalum,
Kaanta chubhne se dard hota kyon hai.

جوشؔ

دِل بے کسیٔ ادب پہ تھرّاتا ہے
مرطوب فضا میں دم گھٹا جاتا ہے
فردوسی و رُود کی سمجھتا ہُوں اُسے
مصرع بھی مِرا جو آج دُہراتا ہے

معنی کی تب و تاب گھٹاتا ہُوں مَیں
جب حلقۂ الفاظ میں لاتا ہُوں مَیں
صد حیف کہ پِگھلے ہُوئے سونے کو ندیم
تانبے کی زمیں پر بہاتا ہُوں مَیں

باقی نہیں اِک شعور رکھنے والا
صہبائے کہُن سال کا چکھنے والا
کیا اپنے معانی کا مَیں رونا رووٗں
الفاظ نہیں کوئی پرکھنے والا

Josh Malihabadi

My heart shudders at the plight of art,
I feel choked in this humid hot,
I call him Firdausi, consider him Rodki,
If someone can repeat even my verse by heart.

Dil be kasi-e-adab pe tharrata hai,
Martub fizaa mein dum ghuta jaata hai,
Firdausi-o-Rodki samjhta hun use,
Misra bhi mera jo aaj dohraata hai.

As I put my thoughts in the verbal mould,
I distort their meaning, I disturb their soul,
Alas, my friend, through copper channel,
I try to force the molten gold.

Maani ki tab-o-taab ghataata hun main,
Jab halqa-e-alfaaz mein laata hun main,
Sud haif, ke pighle hue sone ko nadeem,
Taanbe ki zameen par bahaata hun main.

Not a man is there with sense and taste
Who will relish old wine, who will appreciate?
Why lament about purport and intent,
Even my words none can evaluate.

Baaqi nahin ik shaoor rakhne waala,
Sahbaa-e-kuhan saal ka chakhne waala,
Kya apne maani ka main rona roun,
Alfaaz nahin koi parkhne waala.

جوش

وہ رشتۂ تسبیح ہیں ہم پھندے ہیں
ہر عیب سے وہ پاک ہیں ہم گندے ہیں
دیکھو وہ نکل رہے ہیں مسجد سے شیوخ
گویا وہ خدا ہیں ہم بندے ہیں

مُفلس کا سبُو بھی سرخوشی کی توہین
مُنعِم کے تلاطُم سے بھی پیدا تمکین
ظلمت بردوش اُدھر ہے صُبح مَولُود
خورشید بکف اِدھر ہے شام تدفین

" ہم دَہر کے ناپختہ خیالوں میں نہیں "
" ہم سینۂ آگہی کے چھالوں میں نہیں "
حیرت ہے کہ ہر بھٹکنے والا اِنسان
کہتا ہے کہ " ہم بھٹکنے والوں میں نہیں "

Josh Malihabadi

They are the strings of sacred beads, we the strangling
    ropes,
They, the faultless angels, we, the dirty rogues;
Behold them coming from the mosque, the priests in a
    row,
As if they are the very God, we the abject folks!

Woh rishta-e-tasbeeh hain, hum phunde hain,
Har aib se woh paak hain, hum gande hain,
Dekho woh nikal rahe hain, masjid se shayokh,
Goya woh Khuda hain, hum bande hain.

A poor man's peg is a breach of peace,
A rich man's noise is music sweet,
Here, birthday morn is darkness-drowned,
There, mourning eve is sunshine-steeped.

Muflis ka sabu bhi sar khushi ki tauheen,
Munim ke talaatam se bhi paidaa tamkeen,
Zulmat bardosh udhar hai subah-e-maulud,
Khursheed ba-kaf idhar hai shaam-e-maddafeen.

"Ours are not immature ways,
"We do not fly in the Wisdom's face,"
All erring men, 'tis strange, would say:
"We aren't those who go astray."

"Hum dahar ke naa pukhta khayaalon mein nahin,
"Hum seena-e-aagahi ke chhalon mein nahin,"
Hairat hai ke har bhatakne waalaa insaan,
Kahta hai, "hum bhatakne waalon mein nahin."

جوش

برسات ہے دِل کو ڈس رہا ہے پانی
فُرقت میں تیری جُھلس رہا ہے پانی
دِل میں کبھی چُبھتا ہے ، کلیجے میں کبھی
آڑا ترچھا برس رہا ہے پانی

پروا نہ کریں گے تازہ آنے والے
دو دِن میں بُھلا دیں گے زمانے والے
گُلزار سے اے بہار، جاتی ہے تو جا
اب ہم بھی ہیں عنقریب جانے والے

یاں چمپئی دھوپ ہے گُلابی سایہ
رہتا ہے سحابِ ابدیّت چھایا
جوش آؤ کہ منتظر ہے بزمِ ارواح
آیا ، یارانِ رفتہ آیا ، آیا

Josh Malihabadi

In this rainy season, water bites the heart,
In your absence, it singes me and scalds,
Now it pierces through my heart, now pricks my guts,
Unchecked the water flows, like slanting, shifting darts.

Barsaat hai dil ko dus raha hai paani,
Furqat mein teri jhulas raha hai paani,
Dil mein kabhi chubhta hai, kaleje mein kabhi,
Aara tirchha baras raha hai paani.

Posterity will not care for you,
The world forgets in a day or two,
You may, if you like, quit the garden, Spring,
We too will go as soon as you.

Parwaah na karenge taaza aane waale,
Do din mein bhula denge zamaane waale,
Gulzaar se, ai bahaar, jaati hai to jaa,
Ab hum bhi hain anqareeb jaane waale.

Jasmine-white the sun-shine here, rose-pink the shades,
A cool protective cloud eternally pervades;
The assembled spirits await you, come sharp, O Josh!
"Yes, yes, I am coming, dear departed mates."

Yaan champaey dhoop hai, gulaabi saaya,
Rahta hai suhaab-e-abdeeat chhaya;
Josh aao ke muntazir hai bazm-e-auraah,
"Aaya, yaaraan-e-rafta, aaya, aaya!"

فیض احمد فیض

متاعِ لوح و قلم چھن گئی تو کیا غم ہے
کہ خونِ دل میں ڈبولی ہیں انگلیاں میں نے
زباں پر مہر لگی ہے تو کیا کہ رکھ دی ہے
ہر اک حلقہ زنجیر میں زباں میں نے

آ گئی فصلِ شگوفوں چاک گریباں والو
سل گئے ہونٹ کوئی زخم سلے یا نہ سلے
دوستو بزم سجاؤ کہ بہار آئی ہے
کھل گئے زخم، کوئی پھول کھلے یا نہ کھلے

ڈھلتی ہے موجِ مے کی طرح رات ان دنوں
کھلتی ہے صبح گل کی طرح رنگ و بو سے پُر
ویراں ہیں جام پاس کرو کچھ بہار کا
دل آرزو سے پُر کرو، آنکھیں لہو سے پُر

FAIZ AHMED FAIZ
(1911-1984)

What matters if from me pen and page have slipped,
In my heart's blood my fingers I've dipped;
Why should I complain if my lips are sealed,
Each link of the chain, I have with a tongue equipped.

Mitaa-e-lauh-e-qalam chhin gai to kya ghum hai,
Ke khun-e-dil mein dabo leen hain ungliaan main ne,
Zabaan pe muhar lagi hai to kya dar hai,
Ke rakh di hai har ik halqa-e-zanjeer mein zabaan main ne.

Tranquil times arrive, O ye frenzied folks!
Sealed are our lips at least, if not our wounds,
Arrange, friends, a festive meet, spring resumes its reign,
Wounds at least have blossomed, if not the blooms.

Aa gai fasal-e-sakun chaak-garebaan waalo,
Sil gaye hont, koi zakham sile ya na sile;
Dosto bazm sajaao ke bahaar aai hai,
Khil gaye zakham, koi phool khile ya na khile.

Nowadays the night flows like the flowing wine,
Colourful, scented, wakes the dawn, like an opening bud,
Abandoned lie the cup and can, mind ye, 'tis spring,
Fill your hearts with yearning, your eyes fill with blood.

Dhalti hai mauj-e-mai ki tarah raat in dinon.
Khilti hai subah-e-gul ki tarah rang-o-boo se pur,
Weeraan hain jaam paas karo kuchh bahaar ka,
Dil aarzoo se pur karo, aankhen lahu se pur.

فیض

اپنے انعامِ حُسن کے بدلے
ہم تہی دامنوں سے کیا لینا
آج فُرقت زدوں پہ لُطف کرو
پھر کبھی صبر آزما لینا

شاعر کا جشن سالگرہ ہے، شراب لا
منصب، خطاب، رُتبہ، اُنھیں کیا نہیں ملا
بس نقص ہے تو اِتنا، کہ ممدوح نے کوئی
مصرعہ کِسی کتاب کے شایاں نہیں لکھا

ضبط کا عہد بھی ہے، شوق کا پیماں بھی ہے
عہد و پیماں سے گذر جانے کو جی چاہتا ہے
درد اِتنا ہے کہ ہر رگ میں ہے محشر بر پا
اور سکوں ایسا کہ مر جانے کو جی چاہتا ہے

Faiz

What can we, the indigent, offer in return,
For the prize of beauty which we want to earn,
Be thou kind today to the severance-singed,
You can test our patience at some later turn.

Apne inaam-e-husn ke badle,
Hum tahi daamanon se kya lena,
Aaj furqat zadon pe lutaf karo,
Phir kabhi sabar aazma lena.

It's the birthday of the poet, bring the wine and glass,
Honours, titles, rich awards—what all he didn't amass?
In one respect alone was the worthy man flawed,
He didn't write a single line worthy of applause.

Shaair ka jashan-e-saalgarah hai, sharaab la,
Munsib, khitaab, rutba, inhen kya nahin mila;
Bas nuqs hai to itna, ke mamdooh ne koi,
Misra kisi kitaab ke shaayaan nahin likha.

I'm pledged to self-restraint, I'm intent on love,
I should defy, now I feel, both intent and pledge;
Every vein is splitting with pain, so acute is ache,
So deep is peace indeed, I crave for death.

Zubt ka ahad bhi hai, shauq ka paimaan bhi hai,
Ahd-o-paimaan se guzar jaane ko ji chaahta hai,
Dard itna hai ke har rag mein hai mahshar barpa,
Aur sakun aisa ke mar jaane ko ji chaahta hai.

فیضؔ

دیدہَ تر پہ وہاں کون نظر کرتا ہے
کاسۂ چشم میں خونِ جگر لے کے چلو
اب اگر جاؤ پئے عرضِ طلب اُنکے حضور
دستِ کشکول نہیں، کاسۂ سر لے کے چلو

فکرِ سُود و زیاں تو چھُوٹے گی
مِنّتِ ایں و آں تو چھُوٹے گی
خیر دوزخ میں مَے ملے یا نہ ملے
شیخ صاحب سے جاں تو چھُوٹے گی

وقفِ حرمان و یاس رہتا ہے
دل ہے کہ اکثر اُداس رہتا ہے
تمُ تو غم دے کے بھُول جاتے ہو
مُجھ کو احساں کا پاس رہتا ہے

Faiz

Who is there even to care for your tearful eye,
Charge these cups with the heart's blood, when next
   thither you hie,
Instead of the begging bowl, take your head in hand,
When you go to plead your case, or for her grace apply.

Deeda-e-tar pe wahaan kaun nazr karta hai,
Kaasa-e-chashm mein khunaab-e-jigar le ke chalo;
Ab agar jaao paye arz-e-talab un ke hazur,
Dast-o-kushkaul nahin, kaasa-e-sar le ke chalo.

I'll at least get rid of the fear of loss and gain,
I'll be relieved of beseechings in vain,
Never mind if in hell I'm denied the foaming wine,
The Sheikh at least will not be there to cause me endless
   pain.

Fikar-e-sood-o-zayaan to chhutegi,
Mannat-e-een-o-aan to chhutegi,
Khair dozakh mein mai mile na mile,
Sheikh saahib se jaan to chhutegi.

With grief and gloom remains obsessed,
Oft this heart feels depressed;
You give the ache, and forget,
I remain for aye in debt.

Waqf-e-hirmaan-o-yaas rahta hai,
Dil hai ke aksar udaas rahta hai,
Tum tau ghum deke bhul jaate ho,
Mujhko ahsaan ka paas rahta hai.

فیض

رات یُوں دل میں تِری کھوئی ہوئی یاد آئی
جیسے ویرانے میں چُپکے سے بہار آجائے
جیسے صحراؤں میں ہَولے سے چلے بادِ نسیم
جیسے بیمار کو بے وجہ قرار آجائے

صُبح پھُوٹی تو آسماں پہ تِرے
رنگ رُخسار کی پھُہار گِری
رات چھائی تو رُوئے عالَم پر
تیری زُلفوں کی آبشار گِری

نہ آج لُطف کر اِتنا کہ کل گُذر نہ سکے
وہ رات جو کہ تِرے گیسوؤں کی رات نہیں
یہ آرزو بھی بڑی چیز ہے، مگر ہمدم
وصالِ یار فقط آرزو کی بات نہیں

Faiz

Yesternight your memory stole into my heart,
Like the spring come unawares o'er barren paths,
Like the breeze quietly blowing in the desert wilds,
Like a sick man reviving without apparent cause.

Raat yun dil mein tiri khoi hui yaad aai,
Jaise weeraane mein chupke se bahaar aa jaae,
Jaise sahraaon mein haule se chale baad-e-naseem,
Jaise beemaar ko be wajah qaraar aa jaae.

As the day arose the sky was sprayed,
With the tinted shower of your glowing face,
As the night arrived, on the earth did fall,
Your scented locks, dropping in cascades.

Subah phooti to aasmaan pe tere,
Rung-e-rukhsaar ki phoohaar giri,
Raat chhaai to roo-e-aalam par,
Teri zulfon ki aabshaar giri.

Fete me not with joy today, lest I find it hard
To spend the morrow-night, unsheltered by your locks;
This longing is a thing of worth, yet, I fear, O dear,
Bliss of union lies beyond mere wishful thought.

Na aaj lutaf kar itna ke kal guzar na sake,
Woh raat jo ke tere gaisuon ki raat nahin,
Yeh aarzoo bhi bari cheez hai, magar humdum,
Wisaal-e-yaar faqt aarzoo ki baat nahin.

فیض

یہ خون کی مہک ہے کہ لبِ یار کی خوشبو
کس راہ کی جانب سے صبا آتی ہے دیکھو
گلشن میں بہار آئی کہ زنداں ہوا آباد
کس سمت سے نغموں کی صدا آتی ہے دیکھو

نہ دید ہے نہ سخن، اب نہ حرف ہے نہ پیام
کوئی بھی حیلۂ تسکیں نہیں اور آس بہت ہے
اُمیدِ یار، نظر کا مزاج، درد کا رنگ
تم آج کچھ بھی نہ پوچھو کہ دل اُداس بہت ہے

میخانوں کی رونق ہیں، کبھی خانقہوں کی
اپنا لی ہوس والوں نے جو رسم چلی ہے
دلداریٔ واعظ کو ہمیں باقی ہیں ورنہ
اب شہر میں ہر رندِ خراباتِ ولی ہے

Faiz

Is it the scent of blood, or the fragrance of her lips?
From which side, tell me, bloweth the breeze;
Is it the spring revived, or a prison come alive,
Whence do these strains, mark ye, proceed?

Yeh khoon ki mahak hai ke lab-yaar ki khushboo,
Kis raah ki jaanib se sabaa aati hai dekho,
Gulshan mein bahaar aai ke zindaan hua aabaad,
Kis simt se naghmon ki sadaa aati hai, dekho.

No glimpse, no converse, no word, no news,
No means of solace, yet I hope and trust,
Desire of union, tint of pain, or a hint of glance,
Forget about everything, I feel depressed.

Na deed hai na sakhun, ab na haraf hai, na payaam,
Koi bhi heela-e-taskeen nahin aur aas bahut hai,
Umeed-e-yaar, nazr ka mizaaj, dard ka rung,
Tum aaj kuchh bhi na puchho, ke dil udaas bahut hai.

Now they would grace a tavern, now a hermitage,
Sensual folk are quick to ape whatever be the rage;
We alone are left to brave the preacher's barbs,
Every drunkard masquerades as a holy sage.

Mai khaanon ki raunaq hain, kabhi khanqahon ki,
Apna li hawas waalon ne jo rasam chali hai,
Dildaari-e-waaiz ko hameen baaqi hain, warna,
Ab shahar mein har rind-e-kharaabaat wali hai.

نریش کمار شاد

زندگی کے گھنے اندھیرے میں
ماہ و انجم کا کام دیتے ہیں
لوگ اپنی زبان میں جن کو
جام و مینا کا نام دیتے ہیں

حُسنِ احساس کی ضرورت ہے
ذرّہ ذرّہ حسین مُورت ہے
تیری نظریں ہیں بے بصر ورنہ
زندگی اب بھی خُوبصورت ہے

زندگی شُغلِ آہ و زاری ہے
زندگی ایک ضربِ کاری ہے
پھر بھی کیا دِل کشی ہے ظالم میں
پھر بھی کمبخت کتنی پیاری ہے

NARESH KUMAR SHAD
(1927-1969)

In the life's deepening dark,
They serve as moon and stars,
What in common parlance,
We term as cup and flask.

Zindagi ke ghane andhere mein,
Maah-o-anjam ka kaam dete hain,
Log apni zabaan mein jinko,
Jaam-o-meena ka naam dete hain.

If you have a sensitive heart,
Every grain is a piece of art,
But for your blinkered eyes,
Life is still a beauteous mart.

Husn-e-ahsaas ki zaroorat hai,
Zarra zarra hasin moorat hai,
Teri nazren hain be basar warna,
Zindagi ab bhi khubsoorat hai.

Life with sighs and cries is fraught,
A grievous wound that healeth not,
Attractive yet is this despot,
The wretched thing is dearly sought.

Zindgi shagul-e-aah-o-zaari hai,
Zindgi ek zarb-e-kaari hai,
Phir bhi kya dilkashi hai zaalim mein,
Phir bhi kambakht kitni payaari hai.

شاد

احساس کی زنجیر ہلا دیتا ہے
جذبات میں ہلچل سی مچا دیتا ہے
دھوئے ہوئے مہتاب کی ضَو پاشی ہے
یہ کون میری نیند اُڑا دیتا ہے

تسکین کے اسباب نہیں ہوتے ہیں
لمحے گلِ شاداب نہیں ہوتے ہیں
مَے پینے کو پیتا ہوں مگر غم کی طرح
محفل میں جب احباب نہیں ہوتے ہیں

شیخ صاحب مقابلہ کیسا
آپ کا ہم شراب نوشوں سے
ایک عِصمت فروش بہتر ہے
آپ جیسے خدا فروشوں سے

Shad

Someone shakes the roots of my feeling heart,
Causes deep commotion in my inmost parts,
Who, with the beam of his dazzling moon,
Puts my sleep to flight, makes me feel distraught?

Ahsaas ki zanjeer hila deta hai,
Jazbaat mein halchul si macha deta hai,
Dhoe hue mahtaab ki zau paashi se,
Yeh kaun meri neend ura deta hai.

Ways of contentment cannot be found,
Moments will not blossom on this barren ground,
Albeit I drink, but as with swallowing grief,
I drink all by myself, when friends are not around.

Taskin ke asbaab nahin hote hain,
Lamhe gul-e-shaadaab nahin hote hain,
Mai peene ko peeta hun, magar ghum ki tareh,
Mahfil mein jab ahbaab nahin hote hain.

O Sheikh, what is there to compare,
Between us the drinkers, and you,
An honour-seller is better far
Than he who sells his God, as you.

Sheikh sahib muqaabla kaisa,
Aap ka hum sharab noshon se,
Ek ismat farosh behtar hai,
Aap jaise Khuda faroshon se.

شاد

نکہتوں کا فِشار کہتے ہیں
رحمتِ کردگار کہتے ہیں
آپ کے گیسوؤں کا سایا ہے
لوگ جس کو بہار کہتے ہیں

ساز کے دل میں سوز پلتا ہے
مُسکراہٹ میں درد ڈھلتا ہے
حُسن ہے ایسے اِک چراغ کی لَو
عشق کا جس میں خُون جلتا ہے

دُنیا ہے اِرم سے بھی حسیں دیکھ ذرا
آکاش پہ ہنستی ہے زمیں دیکھ ذرا
آب آب ہوئے جاتے ہیں ماہ و انجم
نَو دیتی ہے ذرّوں کی جبیں دیکھ ذرا

Shad

'Tis the spirit of scents sublime,
'Tis the grace of God divine;
The shade provided by your locks,
Is what they call spring benign.

Nikhaton ka fishaar kahte hain,
Rahmat-e-Kirdgaar kahte hain;
Aapke gaisuon ka sayaa hai,
Log jisko bahaar kahte hain.

In the strings of music pain doth sleep.
Sighs with smiles company keep;
Beauty is the light of such a lamp,
The blood of love which drinketh deep.

Saaz ke dil mein soz palta hai,
Muskraahat mein dard dhalta hai;
Husn hai aise ik chiraagh ki lau,
Ishq ka jismen khoon jalta hai.

More beauteous than heaven is the earth below,
How it mocks the sky, behold!
The moon and stars are flushed with shame,
The grains of dust emit a glow.

Duniya hai Iram se bhi haseen dekh zara,
Aakaash pe hansti hai zameen dekh zara,
Aab aab hue jaate hain maah-o-anjum,
Lau deti hai zarron ki jabeen, dekh zara.

MY JOURNEY
Selected Urdu Poems
Ali Sardar Jafri

Translated by
Baidar Bakht
&
Kathleen Grant Jaeger

Other Titles on Urdu Poetry
by K. C. Kanda

What the reviewers say...

Kanda's efforts to bring Urdu to a wider readership have to be applauded when the language is being allowed to wither away either through the benign neglect of the authorities or by conscious rejection by the younger generation including Muslims.

The Hindustan Times

Kanda's innate love for Urdu poetry gives his work the much-needed soul that breathes life into something as spiritless an exercise as translation.

The Indian Express

Masterpieces of Urdu Ghazal

"It is a miracle that despite the strait-jacket in which it was enclothed, the ghazal not only survived but flourished through the centuries... I recommend this anthology to lovers of Urdu Poetry."

Khushwant Singh

The protagonists of Urdu language will acknowledge readily the debt of gratitude to Kanda for his pioneering and continuing work of translation from Urdu into English.

Deccan Chronicle, Hyderabad

This book gives an insight into the work of modern Urdu poets of the mid-20th century who occupied the centre stage in India and Pakistan. It comes as a breath of fresh air for Urdu lovers who sometimes feel despondent about the future of their beloved language in the Indian sub-continent." (from the review of Masterpieces of Modern Urdu Poetry, published in Deccan Chronicle, November 22, 1998.